L.A. LOFTS

L.A. LOFTS

by Barbara Thornburg

Foreword by Michelle Ogundehin

Photographs by Dominique Vorillon

CHRONICLE BOOKS
SAN FRANCISCO

Library of Congress Cataloging-in-Publication Data available.

ISBN 0-8118-5172-9

Manufactured in China.

Design by Think Studio, NYC

Distributed in Canada by Raincoast Books
9050 Shaughnessy Street
Vancouver, British Columbia V6P 6E5

10 9 8 7 6 5 4 3 2 1

Chronicle Books LLC
85 Second Street
San Francisco, California 94105

www.chroniclebooks.com

To my mother and father,
and my husband, Andy,
with love always, B.T.

Acknowledgments

I have spent an amazing two years discovering downtown Los Angeles and meeting the new urban pioneers who call it home. My special thanks to the owners who opened their lofts—often on early Saturday mornings—and shared their lives and ideas with me. I am indebted to photographer Dominique Vorillon for his photographs, which capture so beautifully the essence of each loft. Also my thanks for important insights on the dynamics of change gained through discussions with Hamed Badad, Hal Bastian, Loni Blanchard, Richard Carlson, Linda Dishman, Greg Fischer, Tom Gilmore, Jean R. Milant, Jon Peterson, George Rollins, Trudi Sandmeier, Carol Shots, and Paul Solomon.

A number of individuals who assisted me with this project deserve much credit and have my deep gratitude: My colleagues at the *Los Angeles Times*, editor Carla Lazzareschi, who encouraged me to create a loft book, and senior editor Martin Smith, for his enthusiasm and practical tips on how to write a book and have a full-time job, too. My editors at Chronicle, Mikyla Bruder and Lisa Campbell, for guiding me so graciously through my first book. Tim Street Porter, Gray Crawford, Ciji Ware, Michael Webb, and Diane Worthington for taking time with me to navigate the labyrinthine world of book contracts. My sensei, Jim Hayes, for his wisdom and kind instruction, and Emily Young. Tom and Alayna Gray, for writing getaways mixed with long walks in the woods at the Santa Lucia Preserve. My husband, Andy, for his organizational, computer, and business skills par excellence; also, his love, unfailing support, and keen sense of humor. And finally, thanks to my Great Dane Cleo, for insisting on computer breaks and walks under the Hollywood sign overlooking the city I love.

Foreword

I'll never forget the day I first walked into my very own loft. It was on the top floor of a decommissioned synagogue in Shoreditch, London's East End. It had huge windows, no heating, a worn wooden floor, and a bath set underneath a sleeping mezzanine. The toilet was on the landing *outside* the front door; the "kitchen" was an excuse of a counter with a sink in it; and to cap it all, the staircase from the ground floor was vertiginous in the extreme. I shared the building with a concert pianist, a rock musician, and a Nigerian shoe wholesaler. My father thought I had regressed to Studentville; my accountant muttered something along the lines of "Well, I suppose it'll be a challenge." I loved it! I'd swapped a sophisticated pied à terre with superior finishes, well-fitted kitchen, power shower, under-floor heating, and acres of storage for something raw that I could shape to suit myself.

Why the shift? Simply, what I wanted from my living space had changed. For a couple of years, I'd been shuttling regularly between London, where I was then Editor at Large of *U.K. ELLE Decoration*, and Los Angeles, where my lover lived. My London pad was therefore required to be no more, really, than an efficient hotel room. But when the relationship ended, my priorities changed. Back in London more or less full-time, I wanted a home, not a hotel. Hence the loft.

Today we are familiar with the concept of home as an extension of our personalities, a blank canvas on which to express ourselves—what greater compliment, after all, than to have someone walk into your space and declare, "It's so *you*!" We don't want bland, we want personal. Our homes should be, to use a fashion analogy, cut to fit in all the right places. They should be the equivalent of a makes-you-feel-great favorite piece of clothing rather than the starch-stiff, smart number only brought out for interviews and funerals. In other words, *home* should represent comfort and personal expression.

And yet, most living spaces seem designed to shunt us from one predesignated box of a room to another. The typical townhouse—with its front room for receiving guests, another for feeding them in, one for preparation of said food, others only for sleeping in, and so on—seems in many ways unsuited to contemporary life. How many of us really need a separate dining room? Or spend time in a formal front room as opposed to comfy den? And yet, most people (in the West, at least) live in a version of this structural template with its cellular layout and prescriptive functionality.

The loft, by contrast, offers a space in which you can determine not only where to put the furniture but also where to place the walls and even the plumbing! It is the antidote to the upstairs-downstairs hierarchy of the regimented terrace or the boredom of the executive home in the suburbs.

But the eager adoption of the loft as a dwelling place was driven by more than just the ability to determine the floor plan. When we think of lofts, whether in downtown Los Angeles or the East End of London, a few universal images spring to mind—lots of light, high ceilings, open plan arrangements, individuality. These are, in my opinion, the fundamental elements of good architecture—in brief, the ability to manipulate light and space, and a freedom of layout. It's the grandeur of the high-ceilinged piano nobles of Italian Renaissance palazzos meets the steel structure and glass walls of the pioneering Modernist architects of the Bauhaus in the 1930s. Add a pinch of the 1980s industrial aesthetic popularized by U.K. architect Richard Rogers' Lloyds Building in the City of London, or the exposed utilities of his Pompidou Centre in Paris completed, with Renzo Piano, even earlier in the 1970s, and the stage is set. Against this backdrop, lofts, wherever they are, can be appreciated as not a trendy flight of fancy, but part of a home's evolution.

Was there a catalyst for their emergence? In the U.K. it was undoubtedly fueled by a government initiative of Margaret Thatcher—hardly the queen of cool! In the late 1980s she instigated a policy that reclassified industrial properties, putting them in the same rental bracket as offices, which effectively enabled landlords to charge a premium for the inner-city units occupied by dozens of small manufacturers and workshops. Tenants moved rather than pay the exorbitant increases and the landlords dreamt of lucrative, large-scale office utopias. But the global recession of the early 1990s put an end to that and the industrial buildings fell vacant, failing to attract back even the original manufacturers who had since modernized and moved on.

Artists, though, saw potential in these abandoned structures where no one else did. As they are often at the forefront of a new zeitgeist—it is in their psyches to rebel, to push against constraint—it is no surprise that artists led the way in reclaiming the derelict factories, empty warehouses, and depositories and making them home. While part of the attraction was no doubt a strike against conventional society, I also believe they simply had the ability to think laterally and imagine possibility.

But these early (often illegal) loft dwellers got politicians and venture capitalists thinking, too. Whole new areas in unfashionable parts of town were suddenly reconsidered as viable for commercial enterprise. Thus, in the U.K., the artists were swiftly followed by property developers and bankers, who had the money to snap up the buildings, now selling cheap, from the recessionary rubble and pay someone else to renovate them.

The arrival of the developers spawned the rise and rise of "loft lifestyle merchandising," which promised to catapult the buyers directly to the upper echelons of haute style and trendiness—rather missing the point. A movement of individuality in home ownership was ruthlessly appropriated by those seeking a way to make money and buy style. The majority of the subsequent developer fit-outs, unsympathetic to the ideals of the genuine loft, simply carved large spaces into a multitude of profitable boxes and furnished them with "identikit" packages of exposed brick, wooden floors, and island kitchen units with lots of matte black and shiny chrome on display. This was not about loft living as a canvas for personal expression, but a caricature of cool, a bland, white-box stereotype of chic, minimalist, urban life—the like of which was never remotely attainable for real people with possessions, jobs, or children.

There were thankfully some notable exceptions to this rule of profit during the loft rush. The German-born, U.S.-educated art collector and investor Harry Handelsman, who went on to found the Manhattan Loft Company, was one of the first to offer lofts as shells as well as finished units. Inspired by what he saw in the SoHo district of New York, his first project in 1992 was the conversion into 23 apartments of a 1930s print works in Clerkenwell, at the time an unremarkable zone between the thriving West End Theatreland and the rundown East End of London. Marketed as a chance to create the life of your choosing on the doorstep of the city, it was a huge success, and the beginning of a string of similarly innovative, owner-focused projects for Handelsman.

Meanwhile, in the North of England, the Urban Splash group headed by the English entrepreneur Tom Bloxham, was gradually turning squalid backwaters and industrial ruin in Liverpool and Manchester into award-winning developments. And earlier in the mid-1980s, Sir Terence Conran had begun the redevelopment of a clutch of abandoned spice warehouses near Tower Bridge in south London. He effectively created a designer district out of nothing. New dwellers were treated to the very best in Conran-approved furnishings and fixtures; glass bricks played a prominent aesthetic role, as did curved walls and open-plan kitchen-dining-lounging scenarios. The area today is undisputedly chic, with its authentic cobbled streets, views over the Thames, preserved warehouse paraphernalia (think wharfs, hoist arms, platforms, and pulleys adorning many a facade), convenient underground parking for residents, swanky galleries, restaurants, and even a Museum of Design! But the prohibitively high prices of an average apartment rob the area of cultural diversity, that endemic mix vital to any truly vibrant neighborhood.

In London's Shoreditch, a veritable hotbed of loft life, the picture is a little different. The area is geographically situated between several ethnically diverse communities. On one side there is the City of London, the capital's financial center; on another a clutch of predominantly white, working class–occupied housing estates; and on yet another, an Indian Muslim stronghold living alongside a thriving, mostly Jewish-owned garment industry. Although the artists initially attracted by the low rents have been forced farther afield by the reappropriation of their properties by the developers, it still adds up to the sort of multicultural and creative melting pot that fits so well

with the loft-living mentality. Imagine, if you will, an average Friday night cocktail of city boys proving their virility by consuming turbo-spicy vindaloo curries alongside visiting West London socialites out being "adventurous" in the local, newly hip bars. Mix in a few elderly, sari-clad ladies volubly berating their wayward sons for ogling aforementioned socialites and a handful of wannabe gangsters looking for trouble. Heady stuff!

Across the spectrum, the loft has been accepted into modern parlance as something beyond just a hip mode of living. More than just a passing style, lofts are a testimony to the unlimited inspiration of the individual. In most major cities from Berlin to São Paulo they have become emblematic of a vision of alternative housing that, in a time of universally dwindling land supplies, has not only revitalized dispossessed buildings and prompted reexamination of "unfashionable" areas but also, and most importantly, is culturally in tune with what many people want.

Loft style has become more than a literal interpretation of living in a loft; today the term is shorthand for any space you make your own—a statement of self beyond the clothes you wear or the car you drive, something particularly pertinent in Los Angeles. Thus in L.A., the loft ideal, perhaps more so than anywhere else, liberated people from accepted rules about what you had to have at home, or even where that home should be, and was enthusiastically and energetically adopted: lofts effectively gave confirmed urbanites permission to indulge themselves. North African colonial furniture meets a little Gypsy styling? Great! Flowers stencilled on the floor? Fantastic! This was about exploring idiosyncrasies and proudly proclaiming them as personal taste. But then I believe a desire for freedom of expression is probably embedded in the DNA of inhabitants drawn to a city willfully carved from the desert and perched on a fault line—no coincidence that Los Angeles is also home to an industry dedicated to the art of the imagination and dreams. To paraphrase George Bernard Shaw, there are two kinds of people in life: those who see the world as it is and wonder why, and those who imagine the world as it should be and say, "why not?" Architects of their own beautiful and innovative spaces, Los Angeles' loft livers are surely in the latter category, among the most creative imagineers of our time.

—MICHELLE OGUNDEHIN
Editor, *ELLE Decoration*

Introduction

L.A. Lofts is a valentine, an intimate tribute to city dwellers who've risen to new heights of imagination and innovation to create light, airy spaces for themselves, homes above and beyond the ordinary. They are in love with lofts, players in an urban romance that began more than a century ago in the bohemian artists' ateliers of Paris and bloomed anew in the mid-1950s on this side of the Atlantic, when New York artists began to carve out live/work spaces in abandoned factories and warehouses. These free-flowing solutions came to define a uniquely American approach to loft design. Adopted now by adventurous city folk on the West Coast, lofts epitomize the romantic, hip, laidback lifestyle of casual, open-plan living.

In the past, the barren reclaimed spaces usually offered few amenities. When New York City artist

Robert Rauschenberg moved into his Fulton Street loft in early 1950, he had no heat or running water. Two decades later, artist George Rollins moved into a Third Street loft in downtown Los Angeles that had neither toilet nor kitchen (but the rent was right: $75 a month for a 3,000-square-foot space). Nowadays, almost all loft conversions include built-in kitchens and enclosed bathrooms. While the hunt for loft locations was once focused almost exclusively on industrial spaces, now any empty building is fair game: unused fire stations and churches, abandoned banks and subway terminals. Their universal appeal, loft dwellers agree, includes wide-open expanses, high ceilings, and the visceral thrills of exposed pipes and brick and light streaming through rows and rows of windows.

For many loft lovers, there's an element of nostalgia as well. In L.A., for example, stately Beaux Arts and Moderne structures, built in the early twentieth century when downtown Los Angeles was Southern California's economic and cultural epicenter, resonate with history. Then there's the attraction of space as blank canvas. As one downtown loft enthusiast explained: "You can build an environment totally on your own terms. You're not inheriting someone else's vision."

L.A. Lofts defines L.A.-style loft living through photographs of adaptively reused or specially designed buildings and their vibrant, imaginative interiors. Although the definitions overlap, there are essentially three types of lofts represented here. The traditional open-plan loft, typically favored by artists, includes such spaces as those in the Brewery and the Santa Fe Art Colony, two of downtown L.A.'s earliest loft communities. "Demi-lofts" constructed in early twentieth-century commercial buildings in the city's Historic Core, such as the 1907 San Fernando Building, include loft elements in apartment-like spaces. Finally, there is the rising generation of brand-spanking-new lofts, often tricked out with luxuries such as high-end appliances, granite-topped counters, and bath-cum-spa tubs. Typical of these are the Lofts at Melrose Place in West Hollywood, with similar developments mushrooming elsewhere in Los Angeles and across the United States. Nouveau, industrial-looking structures set in upscale areas, they offer a host of amenities for those who love the loft aesthetic but not the urban-gritty lifestyle.

The first wave of Los Angeles loft residents established themselves in the mid-1970s, nearly two decades after New York City artists had settled in SoHo—the neighborhood between Houston and Canal streets formerly known as Hell's Hundred Acres. Like their New York brethren, these pioneer Angeleno artists were in search of dirt-cheap, spacious spreads in which to work and live. They found niches—often illegally—in abandoned industrial and commercial buildings downtown, such as printing, toy, and garment factories; truck depots; shipping depositories; breweries; and railroad and spice warehouses.

In the late '70s and early '80s, artists flocked in increasing numbers to the downtown area east of Alameda Street, creating a loft neighborhood consequently known as the Arts District. Its nexus at Traction Avenue and Hewitt Street was anchored by Bloom's General Store and Cigar Lounge, the Los Angeles Institute of Contemporary Art, and Lili Lakitch's Gallery of Neon Art. A surreal, multihued airplane perched on the side of the American Hotel above Al's Bar on Hewitt—a bohemian watering hole—was a beacon for the unconventional inhabitants.

Hot on the artists' trail, more than two dozen galleries sprang up in the area, its boosters touting the neighborhood as the future SoHo-West. The City of Los Angeles lent assistance with its adoption of the 1982 Artists in Residence ordinance: Recognizing the growing number of artists living in industrial spaces, the law gave loft dwellers legal residential status. But the lack of certain mainstream amenities thwarted the critical mass needed for the community to flourish; wealthy clients from the outlying neighborhoods failed to venture downtown, and many galleries moved or vanished. Established artists' communities like the Brewery, the Santa Fe Art Colony, and 500 Molino survived, but the downtown arts scene lost much of its glitter, further beleaguered by the 1990 recession, and the Rodney King riots in 1992.

Fortunately, through it all, arts, preservation, and business-backed organizations persevered. Among the groups promoting downtown with loft openings and exhibitions were Los Angeles Contemporary Exhibitions (LACE), Los Angeles Visual Arts (LAVA), Downtown Artists Development Association (DADA), and the Central City Association. The city's premier preservation group, the Los Angeles Conservancy, introduced hundreds to downtown's attractions and heritage through a series of walking tours.

In 1992, a catalyst arrived from New York in the person of self-made, Pied Piper developer Tom Gilmore. He established the Old Bank District in the heart of L.A.'s Historic Core, turning three fin de siècle buildings—the San Fernando, the Continental, and the Hellman—into loft apartments. By the end of the 1990s, the second wave of loft development in Los Angeles had reached substantial heights.

Adding impetus was the Central City Association's push for more enlightened zoning legislation. The City Council's 1999 Adaptive Reuse ordinance streamlined the process of resuscitating old buildings into live/work spaces, essentially allowing building conversion to bypass the labyrinthine zoning process. Other influences converged. The Los Angeles Conservancy's 1999 Broadway Initiative encouraged and promoted revitalization of the Historic Core. In 2001, the *Los Angeles Times* magazine began to champion the stalwarts who called downtown home. New cultural institutions—Walt Disney

Concert Hall, the Cathedral of the Angels, and the Staples Center sports arena—added force to the urban magnet. Films and advertising played supporting roles: the movies *9½ Weeks* (1986), *Ghost* (1990), and *A Perfect Murder* (1998), as well as television commercials and fashion print ads shot in downtown lofts and surrounding locations, popularized the alternative lifestyle.

Currently in L.A., loft residents have established five major enclaves. The Arts District, bordered by the 101 Freeway on the north, 7th Street on the south, Alameda Street on the west, and the Los Angeles River on the east, is home to more than 2,000 artists. A communal neighborhood ambience lingers in this downtown birthplace of the L.A. loft, with its small pocket of ethnic restaurants, an equity waiver theater, a smattering of art galleries and coffeehouses, and a corner general store.

Loft life is on the rise for professionals in the city's Historic Core, with lofts in the once-vibrant financial and cultural center enclosed by 3rd and 9th streets on the north and south and Main Street and Broadway on the east and west. Along Broadway—the first and largest Historic Theater District to be listed on the National Register of Historic Places—a dozen movie palaces recall downtown's early glory. On Spring Street, banking central in the early part of the twentieth century, the Beaux Arts and Moderne facades boast some of L.A.'s best architectural treasures: the Hellman Building (1904), the Continental Building (1904), the Title Insurance and Trust Company (1928), and the Los Angeles (now Pacific Coast) Stock Exchange (1929).

Industrial Santa Fe Avenue has been reborn as home to adventurous residential spirits and now the Southern California Institute of Architecture. The avenue, bordering the Arts District, is a postapocalyptic warren of old garment and tire factories, barbed wire and chain-link fences, and has few retail amenities; run out of milk and there's no corner store. But SCI-Arc's new campus, at the corner of Third and Santa Fe in a quarter-mile-long railroad freight building, promises to act as a focus for development along a corridor that terminates at the Santa Fe Art Colony at 25th Street.

A favorite among loft devotees, North Main Street's Brewery, a complex developed in the early '80s, still flourishes. Gone are the tanks in which Pabst Blue Ribbon beer was brewed. In their place are about 300 lofts in 21 industrial buildings of concrete, brick, and corrugated metal. Only artists and those in arts-related fields are permitted to reside there, and along with galleries there are on-site amenities from catering services to camera rental to film development. The San Antonio Winery, established in 1917, is two blocks away. It's a concentration of urban cool with a three-year waiting list.

South Park is the newest revitalized neighborhood. Once a sleepy mix of seedy hotels and new and used car dealerships with an inordinate number of parking lots, the area now is home to the Fashion Institute of Design and Merchandising, the Los Angeles Convention Center, and Staples Center. The center draws thousands of sports fans and is the venue for the Emmys and rock concerts by the likes of Madonna, Bruce Springsteen, and U2. Bordered by the Harbor Freeway and Main Street on the west and east and the Santa Monica Freeway on the north and south, a new sports and entertainment development in the area dubbed LA Live—plus a new supermarket— also bodes well for the livelihood of the downtown scene.

Who lives and works in L.A. lofts? Some, to be sure, are fine artists and skilled artisans. But overall, new loft residents are a mix of transplanted urbanites, junior entertainment executives making reverse commutes to Burbank and West Hollywood, Internet entrepreneurs, and people in art-related fields. Many are late-twenty- and thirty-somethings, some are older. They come as singles and as couples, mostly sans children, often with pet companions. Lured by the energy and kaleidoscopic variety of urban living, they eschew the often bland and homogeneous suburban lifestyle of their peers or parents and grandparents. Some lofters are empty nesters who prefer the excitement of a hands-on living space over the predictability of condos, and increasingly, there is a smattering of well-heeled types who see a pied-à-terre as an entrée to a newly fashionable downtown.

L.A. Lofts celebrates the diversity of Southern California living with a detailed look at 20 creative spaces. Most are located in the downtown area, while a few are found in the adjacent communities of West Hollywood and Venice. Decors range from '30s Art Deco and Midcentury Modern to fantasy spaces recalling Gothic castles and Vermont barns. Each story delves into why the residents took the loft leap and how they transformed their spaces to make them their own. This book pays homage to these urban pioneers' personal styles. No cookie-cutter places these: California's do-your-own-thing maxim holds sway, with every loft reflecting the owners' whims, fantasies, and personal passions. As living laboratories, lofts offer a wealth of creative design ideas, such as how to define space through use of color, protect art from harmful ultraviolet rays, or devise creative built-ins and floor, window, and wall treatments. While these and other valuable tips in the pages that follow may inspire those considering the loft life, many are useful for apartment dwellers and house owners as well.

Who would have thought it? A new generation has moved into downtown Los Angeles—condemned for years as a city without a heart—and discovered a Tinseltown romance in an L.A. loft.

Art Deco Digs

ARTHUR & ANTONIA ASTOR

If Jay Gatsby were alive in twenty-first-century Los Angeles, he would be enthralled by the stylish Art Deco penthouse of radio station magnate Arthur Astor and his wife, Antonia. Pedigree Moderne furnishings by David Desky, glass by René Lalique, and artwork by Tamara de Lampicka, Alberto Vargas, and Erté decorate the 2,750-square-foot space. Another striking feature: vintage radios galore. "When you walk in here," says Arthur, a native Angeleno and owner of one of the largest working-radio collections in the world, "you're turning the clock back 70 years."

A dedicated downtowner, Arthur is steeped in memories of Los Angeles' past. He fondly recalls Saturdays spent at his father's Chapman Building office at 8th and Broadway; afternoon visits to the Orpheum Theater; and shopping trips with mom to May Co. and the ultimate Art Deco emporium,

Bullock's Wilshire. "Los Angeles was a focal point in the thirties, forties, and fifties," he says. "All of a sudden there's a magnetism again. I'm back in love with downtown."

Astor was so smitten with the emerging urban neighborhood that when a former high school chum, real estate developer Harlan Lee, transformed the 1936 UPS distribution station across from the Staples Center sports arena into a 91-unit loft complex, he snapped up one of the five penthouses for a family pied-à-terre.

He selected a glass-enclosed corner unit on the fourth story, added by Lee's design team, to the refurbished olive and gold concrete building. The loft's plan is open, with a living room, dining room, kitchen, and bath; a two-bedroom-and-bath mezzanine; and stunning views of the downtown skyline. Furnishings and materials are rendered in a subtle palette of sophisticated hues: gray, brown, black, and ivory, punctuated by color jolts from old Hollywood posters and the vintage radios.

The Astors upgraded the loft's appointments while it was still in the construction phase, adding cherrywood kitchen cabinets and black CaesarStone counters in the kitchen. Blond bamboo flooring now warms the concrete-slab floor and metal-grid stair treads. A white metal staircase and balustrade was repainted black to add drama and complement the Deco decor; gallery-white walls, Arthur says, show off his collections best.

A media center, built into the back wall of the new laundry room, houses his stereo, DVD, and VCR in the bottom half. Above, art books and Art Deco objets d'art mingle. Adjacent to the cherrywood unit, a plasma-screen TV sits flush against the window wall and swings out as needed.

The crowning piece occupies the spacious foyer: a 12-foot-long, three-bay black lacquer cabinet with a chrome reveal by interior designer Janet Carpenter of Artistic Environments. Built along the wall, it holds 40 of Arthur's favorite Catalins, Zeniths, and Majestics from the '20s, '30s, and '40s—all in superb working condition. "Old radios sound different," he says. "The resonance comes from the quality of the wood; when an old radio plays it tingles under your hand."

His most prized specimen is a 1930s Radiobar Co. of America radio that lights up when the cabinet is opened, displaying a sparkling array of glass bottles and cocktail glasses. It conjures Gatsby, mixing a gin martini.

ABOVE: The Astors updated the kitchen with stainless-steel appliances, cherrywood cabinets, black cultured-stone counters, and a gray glass backsplash.

OPPOSITE, TOP: Floor-to-ceiling windows offer sweeping views of the downtown skyline. Two new Art Deco–style mohair-and-wood chairs inspired by 1930s theater lobby seats flank a Zenith long-distance radio, which serves as an end table.

OPPOSITE, BOTTOM: The Astors' Radiobar, with pin-up-girl decals on the mirror, automatically lights up when the doors of the bar are opened.

PAGE 14: Awning-style windows are double-glazed for energy efficiency as well as sound control since the Metro Blue Line passes directly in front of the building. An Art Deco gray suede sofa and pairs of arm chairs sit atop a custom-designed area rug that defines the living room space.

PAGE 15: Developer Harlan Lee hired Santa Monica architect Johannes Van Tilburg of Van Tilburg, Banvard & Soderbergh to transform the former UPS distribution center and one-time home of the Bronson clothing company into ninety-one stylish lofts directly across the street from the Staples Center, home of the L.A. Lakers.

ABOVE: An Art Deco chandelier hangs over a vintage dining room table, chairs, and buffet by David Desky.

OPPOSITE: Arthur hung his collection of vintage Hollywood posters along the stairwell walls. On the floor below, a dozen floor outlets were added to hide cords from torchères and freestanding vintage radios. In addition, an enclosed laundry area was added next to the corner powder room in the entry.

PREVIOUS SPREAD: A new cherrywood-and-glass media center houses entertainment equipment, art books, and Art Deco objects. A plasma screen TV swings out from the window wall when needed.

RAZZLE-DAZZLE FLOOR

The Astors decided to upgrade their penthouse's concrete-slab floors and industrial metal-grid staircase. Seeking a finished appearance, they painted the white metal staircase and railing a dramatic black, then laid a handsome, blond bamboo floor. The bamboo is glued directly to the concrete floor. (For lofts or apartments with a plywood subfloor instead of the more sound-absorbent concrete, acoustic cork can be laid first to deaden sound.) In addition, the 42-inch metal stair treads were fitted with matching bamboo cut to size and set inside the existing metal frames. A bullnose in the same material finishes the stair's edge. A dozen black-head wood screws were drilled directly into the mesh base to secure each tread.

ABOVE: A Tamara de Lampicka painting hangs over a pair of Art Deco twin beds in the upstairs guest bedroom.

LEFT: An Art Deco bed and vanity are protected from harmful ultraviolet rays by black, museum-quality mesh shades controlled electronically.

OPPOSITE: A large custom cabinet designed in an Art Deco style houses Astor's large collection of tabletop radios. At the end of the foyer hall, a corner powder room butts up against a new laundry/storage area.

Country Home in the City

JOANNE & FRED BALAK

If it weren't for the concrete floors and fluted columns running down the center of the room in artist Joanne and Fred Balak's home, you might think you were in a converted barn in Pennsylvania's Bucks County instead of a loft at Factory Place on the border of Los Angeles' produce market. Hook rugs, homemade furniture, slipcovered sofas, and cow ephemera combine to create the shabby chic farmhouse style. The Balaks find nothing incongruous about their "country home in the city." "We've always loved the look," Joanne Balak says. "It's very comfortable and warm."

Many of the Early American and Shaker-style furnishings decorated their former home of 26 years, a Mediterranean-style triplex overlooking Century City. Attached as they were to their Westside digs, the Balaks long had dreamed of living and working in a loft. When their son left home, they abandoned the comfort zone of their fashionable neighborhood to concentrate on their art, moving downtown to a 1920s building that had housed a card- and paper-manufacturing plant.

The five-story building, located between the Three Star Smoked Fish Co. and the Los Angeles Gun Club, seemed ideal. They did have to get used to the squeal of car chases being filmed on the nearby 6th Street Bridge and the roaring of produce trucks at 3:00 a.m. "Ear plugs," Fred Balak says, "helped a lot."

They rented a 2,500-square-foot space on the fourth floor of the dark turquoise building, now home to 65 artists' lofts. The landlord agreed to paint the rust brown concrete floor a neutral gray and whitewash the walls. The Balaks did everything else.

A woodworker and furniture maker, Fred Balak built his own partition walls and furnishings. He began by enclosing a 12-by-15-foot space near the center of the room, behind the old elevator shaft, for the master bedroom. Two-by-fours bolted to the cement floors frame 7-foot-high walls; shelves added between the studs create narrow ledges for small art objects and pictures. A walnut-framed window he found discarded in a Santa Monica alley, now mounted in the wall, brings in light, air, and occasional moon views. The outside of the bedroom walls are covered in bead board, in keeping with the country-house motif.

Fred Balak added another bedroom across from the master and set in a small home office within the three remaining cement walls of the former elevator shaft. Joanne took the area at the far end near the south-facing windows for her painting studio, and painted accent walls throughout the loft in yellow, green, and barn red.

Only the kitchen, assigned to the left of the entry, remained to be designed and built. They kept an existing sink on the back wall, then added new pine shelves and distressed-birch plywood cabinets. Fred made a large center island from the bottom of a Hoosier cabinet, a large, all-purpose work center from the early 1900s. Known for his dessert making, he topped the island with a counter of granite and butcher block, "good," he says, "for rolling out pastry on one side and chopping on the other." The large island holds kitchen paraphernalia, and gives the couple additional counter space and a place for casual dining.

Guests sit at the painted dining table on unmatched vintage chairs in front of a sideboard fashioned in part from an old factory workbench. "Fred's made nearly every piece of furniture in the place," Joanne says, "*and* he bakes a killer lemon cake." Her husband adds: "It's all part and parcel of our country-cottage ambience."

ABOVE: If it weren't for the concrete floors and fluted columns down the center of the room, you could be in a converted barn in Pennsylvania instead of a loft at Factory Place.

OPPOSITE, TOP: A pair of slipcovered sofas scattered with pillows flank a built-in bookcase wall. Fred's office is located in the former shell of the freight elevator behind the wall.

OPPOSITE, BOTTOM: The couple leave each other messages on the blackboard on the small desk, adjacent to the dining room.

PAGE 24: The Balaks' entry table, a West L.A. alley find, had a top with only one leg when they found it. Fred duplicated the other legs and added a stretcher support; Joanne painted the decorative top. On the wall: Joanne's painting of a young girl; a pair of Shaker-style sock forms; an array of folk art carvings; and an old cheese mold.

PAGE 25: Factory Place, a five-story building in the Arts District, is home to 65 artists' lofts.

ABOVE: Originally, only a sink existed in the kitchen. Fred built in all the cabinetry, shelves, and the large center island.

OPPOSITE: A weathered dining table is surrounded by mismatched vintage chairs painted in pairs of gray, white, and black. Fred made the buffet from a discarded workbench. He crafted the wood-and-corrugated-metal top, then painted and weathered it to match the bottom.

SHABBY CHIC FINISH

Fred Balak transforms found objects into shabby chic furnishings by combining old and new pieces. To create an overall distressed patina, he begins by beating the wood with chains of differing link sizes. Poking holes with a sharp pick replicates worm borings; a knife-like tool produces scarring. After beating, stabbing, and slashing the furniture, Balak applies a dark stain. To achieve the gray patina for their dining room buffet (half of which is new wood, the other half an old factory workbench), he dry-brushed the surface with gray water-based acrylic, using inexpensive brushes dipped in paint, then wiped off. Painting with a barely loaded "dry" brush in this manner allows the stain to show through. After the paint dries, a light sanding reveals additional glimpses of the dark under-coat. The finishing touch: a coat of Briwax and a good rubbing with a soft rag.

ABOVE, TOP: Joanne took the area near a row of south-facing windows for her colorful painting studio.

ABOVE, BOTTOM: The Balaks' master bedroom is located behind the walls of Joanne's studio/office.

OPPOSITE: Fred framed in a master bedroom with low-rising, 7-foot-tall walls to bring in air and light from south-facing windows. Niches in the walls serve as display areas for small collectibles.

Chinatown Pied-à-Terre

LONI BLANCHARD

When Loni Blanchard found it in 1995, the People-People cooking factory and restaurant on secluded Bamboo Lane had been abandoned for nearly a decade. Commercial refrigerators and stoves languished in the corners and old food containers littered the floors. The electricity and plumbing didn't work. The roof leaked. The basement was always musty and damp; rain turned it into a pond.

Blanchard, an attorney and real estate developer, had spied the two-story, 1950s building on a drive through Chinatown and thought it would be perfect for a downtown office and pied-à-terre. "I just saw this beautiful old concrete industrial building," he recalls. "I thought it had great loft potential. I knew I could fix up the rest."

Blanchard began by removing the exterior wood siding, replacing it with grayish green corrugated metal. He added a new storefront window on the first floor and a small curio window in the hall stairwell—former site of the restaurant's take-out window. He kept the five steel-sash, tilt-out windows on the second floor where his office would go.

With an updated facade and a new roof to keep out the rain, he turned his attention to reconfiguring the space. Because of the concrete-and-steel construction, there were almost no interior bearing walls, he says. As a result, Blanchard could arrange the 3,750-square-foot interior any way he wanted.

He gutted the interior except for the poured-concrete stairs and kept the main floor as a public area. He built a small gallery off the entry across from the stairs, followed by a dining room, kitchen, and bath. Black canvas-covered plywood walls on tracks slide out and close off the dining room. Similar doors partition off a pantry opposite the kitchen.

Upstairs, he placed his office at the front of the building, overlooking the Good Health Adult Day Care Center. He added an enclosed library right outside his office; between the library and a small storage room and bath at the rear, he created a reception area. With no windows, the basement proved an ideal location for his art storage area as well as a quiet spot for his bedroom.

His extensive collection of black-and-white photographs and contemporary paintings is juxtaposed with Melanesian spirit masks, African sculptures, and modern furnishings by Mies van der Rohe, Eileen Gray, and Herman Miller. In the mix are Blanchard's own creations, including a 2,000-pound ebony-stained concrete dining table. A host of crosses decorate his office. "They're all romantic symbols for me," he says, "things that make me feel good."

These things include Asian food, and of course Blanchard has dozens of choices nearby. Dim sum at the Empress in the building across the street is his personal favorite. "I've always had a passion for Chinese restaurants," he says.

ABOVE: Blanchard resurfaced and sealed the restaurant's original concrete floor. He installed disco balls at either end of the hall to bounce light into the interior space.

RIGHT: Charles Eames aluminum group chairs surround Blanchard's kitchen table.

OPPOSITE, TOP: Blanchard bought unfinished cabinets from a discount retail store, painted them dark brown, then poured concrete countertops on site. He finished the homemade pine table with opaque deck paint in the same hue. Three floor-to-ceiling pantry doors slide away for easy access to food, dishes, and kitchen supplies.

OPPOSITE, BOTTOM: A triangular New Guinea house mask hangs behind Blanchard's custom concrete-and-glass desk.

PAGE 32: Blanchard's dining room features a monolithic, poured-in-place concrete dining/conference table that weighs in at 2,000 pounds. The weathered-looking finish is a combination of sanded silver paint, ebony concrete stain, and clear sealer. A pair of canvas-covered plywood panels set on tracks slide out to enclose the dining room.

PAGE 33: Blanchard added a new storefront window on the first floor of the former Chinese restaurant and changed the wood siding to corrugated metal. He kept the row of tilt-out windows overlooking the alley in his upstairs office.

INDUSTRIAL ART SHELF

Blanchard, who calls himself the "poster child for Home Depot," used 1-by-4-inch aluminum channels—normally doorjamb parts—to create shallow ledges for displaying photographs and other small artwork in his library. He hung two 10-foot-long channels on opposite walls at staggered heights. Chromed wood screws driven into studs hold the narrow shelves in place. Blanchard thought he could simply lean the art against the wall but soon found it wasn't secure enough. He added chromed metal screws with ½-inch heads behind each artwork, leaving the screws slightly protruding. He then looped a large rubber band around the wire-backed frame of each piece and looped the other end around the screw. His solution keeps the art firmly held in place, and he hopes his displays will withstand California's next temblor.

ABOVE: Blanchard decorated the office with his collections of crosses and ethnic and modern art; modern black leather furnishings sit atop a sisal area rug.

OPPOSITE: Blanchard used inexpensive aluminum channels screwed into wall studs to hold his collection of black-and-white photographs. An old Italian fruitwood workbench serves as his library table.

ABOVE: Blanchard placed his bedroom downstairs in the windowless basement, which offers a quiet, peaceful retreat. A traditional sleigh bed keeps company with a vintage Marcel Breuer B35 chair and a contemporary painting by James Mathers.

LEFT: A small second-floor bathroom at the rear of the loft features a concrete sink and a black-canvas, swivel-mounted privacy partition.

OPPOSITE: Blanchard added a concrete koi pond and small spray fountain in the courtyard at the rear of his loft.

Feng Shui Haven

KENNETH BROWN

Interior designer and television host Kenneth Brown's Westside loft is not your typical raw artist's space. True, the three-story, bow-truss building of cinder block and corrugated metal looks like it would be at home near train tracks and loading docks. And true, the interior's concrete floor, exposed ducts and pipes, and industrial garage door are familiar loft elements.

Its main distinction from the average reused-industrial space: it's brand-spanking-new. The kitchen is outfitted with GE Monogram appliances and a Sub-Zero refrigerator. The bathroom walls are clad in sleek limestone and Venetian glass tiles. No urban grit here, but rather, appointments befitting artsy West Hollywood, hub of Los Angeles' design center and fashionable restaurants.

But for all its sleek fixtures and chic setting, the 1,800-square-foot space, Brown says, needed an infusion of "good energy." He works hectic 15-hour days shooting his show and running a busy interior design business. What Brown and business partner Matthew Rachleff wanted most, they said, was a "tranquil retreat."

In pursuit of this soothing equilibrium, Brown sought out a master of feng shui, the ancient Chinese practice of creating a flow of positive energy between the elements: stone, wood, metal, earth, wind, and fire. The expert he found, Katherine Anne Lewis, counseled replacing the concrete floors with African walnut. The wood, she said, balances the harsh, exposed building materials of the loft's air-conditioning ducts, PVC pipes, and metal stairs. In the kitchen, new Madagascar ebony cabinets offset heavy-gauge stainless-steel countertops; a large travertine backsplash brings in an earth element. Brown says the music implicit in the grand piano near the entry stimulates the energy in his "career corner," and a large amethyst next to the bed "ensures wealth."

After addressing the critical "harmony" quotient, Brown turned his attention to dividing up the 1,800-square-foot space. He enclosed a small area next to the entrance for an office, then created a master bedroom suite at the opposite end. In both rooms he added large crown moldings—"to outline the spaces and make them more elegant," he says. He left the main room open: the living room area is next to a roll-up windowed garage door overlooking the street; the dining room floats in the middle of the loft between the office and the kitchen.

Furnishing the new loft, Brown worked in his characteristic style: traditional with a pared-down modern aesthetic. "The warmth and comfort of the traditional is for me a legacy of growing up in a plantation-style home in Baton Rouge, Louisiana," he says. Many of the furnishings he designed are in a mix of beautiful woods: a 10-foot-tall cherrywood headboard, zebrawood night tables, a rift oak–and-mahogany dining table.

Walls and windows covered with soft wool and ebony-stained floors create the perfect foil for the sofas and chairs in natural, earth-tone fabrics—linen and cotton, silk and suede. "I wanted the loft to feel like a tailored man's suit," Brown says, "elegant, sexy, and so comfortable you could sleep in it. And of course, full of positive energy."

ABOVE: Brown installed a new soffit in the living room ceiling to hide the industrial garage door when it rolls up. "The look was just a little too raw for me," he says. The custom drapes are made of the same soft wool used for the wall covering.

OPPOSITE: Brown added warmth and luxury to the living room by covering the walls in a men's suit fabric.

PAGE 40: When Brown couldn't find a painting he liked for this space, he painted an abstract canvas himself, picking up the loft's earth-toned palette.

PAGE 41: The three-story industrial-looking "new loft" is located in a tony area of West Hollywood adjacent to Melrose Place.

ABOVE: Brown's office, installed near the entry, overlooks the bamboo-and-steel corridor of the 12-unit condominium.

OPPOSITE: Ebony cabinets and a stainless-steel countertop set off the new African walnut floors replaned to give a hand-hewn finish.

PREVIOUS SPREAD: Brown's rift oak-and-mahogany dining table surrounded by Michael Rudin chairs sits in the center of the loft between the kitchen and office. The dining table is multi-functional, also serving as a game and buffet table.

PERSONALIZED BATHROOM

Brown spruced up his office bathroom by painting horizontal stripes above the Venetian glass wainscot. After painting the walls in dark taupe, he divided the space into five 16-inch stripes using a chalk line and masking tape, then completed the design by alternating light taupe with the dark. To reinforce the horizontal theme, he painted a long abstract landscape on a two-by-four and hung it on the wall. "The banding creates visual movement in the room," he says, "and makes it appear larger." To further personalize the space, he replaced the conventional white pedestal sink with a farmers sink set atop a vintage Asian cabinet. Holes drilled through the top and back of the black lacquer cabinet create access to connect the plumbing.

ABOVE: For the office bathroom, Brown painted a horizontal landscape to hang atop the wall he'd decorated with bands of light and dark taupe. He replaced the standard pedestal sink with a farmers sink set atop a Chinese cabinet.

OPPOSITE: Brown designed a dramatic 10-foot-tall cherrywood headboard with chrome inlays. He topped his zebrawood night table with a vintage Murano glass lamp; an Indian silk comforter covers the bed.

North African Colonial Meets Camargue Gypsy

DENISE DOMERGUE

Art conservator Denise Domergue was ready for a lifestyle change. Her 1920s Larchmont cottage was charming, to be sure, but she was beginning to feel claustrophobic. "I wanted to burst out psychologically as well as physically," says the restorer of nineteenth- and twentieth-century paintings. When a friend's loft in Venice became available, Domergue sold her home and moved to the bohemian seaside community.

The vine-covered facade of the '60s-era redwood-sided building exudes a charm that had attracted a succession of artist tenants. Although the building is set back from the street, Domergue commissioned a sculptural steel gate to ensure privacy and security in this busy neighborhood—a mix of antique shops and graffiti-choked alleyways.

Domergue took the 1,800-square-foot upper level of the two-story building as living quarters for herself and her teenage son, Axel. She called in Los Angeles designer Jackie Terrell of Jackie Terrell Design and Venice designer Kate Meigneux of Meigneux + Keer Studios to help reconfigure the space. Originally, the 60-foot-long loft was open, with a rudimentary kitchen and a single partition wall; a bedroom and bathroom now anchor opposite ends. In between are an open living room, kitchen, dining room, sitting room, and library/office. Downstairs, about one-third of the space serves as Domergue's studio. The remainder is leased to an architect.

To get full use of the interiors, Domergue built a mezzanine under the 16-foot-tall ceiling. Located directly above her son's bedroom and outfitted with a pair of twin mattresses and scads of pillows, the room functions as "Axel's lounge," and, occasionally, a guest bedroom. Six skylights bathe the interior in natural light. Inexpensive aluminum sliding glass doors at the front entrance and master bedroom have been replaced with large French doors, which open onto a spacious deck. A galley kitchen with a center island opposite the entry serves as the loft's focal point. "I love to stand in the kitchen with the door open to catch the ocean breeze," she says, "and watch the big wet cloud formations roll in."

From her kitchen-island perch, Domergue's home is awash in color. Designer Jackie Terrell dreamed up the upbeat color scheme. Individual walls are in hues of willow green and raspberry. In the bedroom she combined two walls striped in periwinkle blue and acid yellow with another awash in deep pumpkin. "I wanted color," Domergue says, "to give each space its own identity."

Domergue's furnishings and collections are eclectic in a style she calls "North African colonial meets Camargue gypsy." In the bedroom there's a toile de Jouy slipcovered daybed, an Indian wool throw, an embroidered Spanish shawl tablecloth, and a floral needlepoint bergère. A pair of Indonesian tables in the dining room are surrounded by Arne Jacobsen and Art Deco cane chairs. A quartet of thrift store horns—greater kudo, sable antelope, and Thompson's gazelle—hang overhead.

The crazy-quilt look extends to the bathroom, formerly a bland little kitchen but now all aglow with robin's-egg blue cabinets and colorful accessories. "And," Domergue hastens to say, "I haven't finished yet." For the conservator there's really no downside to living in a loft. "The older I get," she says, "the more space, air, and openings I want."

ABOVE: Arne Jacobsen and slipcovered Art Deco cane chairs surround a pair of Indonesian tables. Various deer horns Domergue found at a local thrift shop are mounted on the dining room's pea-soup green wall.

OPPOSITE, TOP: The galley kitchen features a center island topped with a pumpkin-colored cultured stone counter, a backsplash of yellow and red Moroccan tiles, and medium-density fiberboard (MDF) cabinets painted in dill pickle green.

OPPOSITE, BOTTOM: A large window overlooking an alley in Domergue's office/library has been replaced with a wall of book-shelves to house her large collection of art books.

PAGE 50: A pair of white denim love seats flanks a wall painted with Benjamin Moore's raspberry truffle in Domergue's sitting room. A Frank Gehry corrugated cardboard Little Beaver chair and ottoman and a French willow chair add the mix of eclectic seating. Overhead hangs a Bob Wilheit paper-and-balsa sculpture.

PAGE 51: Domergue's two-story redwood-clad building features a small fountain in the front courtyard.

DEX-O-TEX DELIGHT

Originally, Domergue envisioned farmhouse planks covering her loft's plywood subfloor. To prepare the floor, she hand-troweled on a polymer coating called Dex-O-Tex. The smooth, seamless coating is often used as an underlayment for outdoor decks and other surfaces. She liked the results so much, she left it uncovered. The coating is available in off-the-shelf colors ranging from beiges, gold, and grays to a variety of reds, blues, and greens; Domergue and Terrell customized their own lettuce hue. The cool color acts as a perfect foil for her eclectic furnishings and art. In the master bathroom, the linoleum-like surface of the polymer abuts bright blue cobalt tile. Domergue says the surface is a wonderful alternative to the cold, concrete-slab floors typical of lofts—and, most importantly, is easy to clean.

ABOVE: Domergue put a master bathroom on the site of the former tenant's makeshift kitchen. Eschewing traditional bathroom counters, she used vintage cabinets. A branch mirror, painted to resemble coral, hangs above the commercial sink and faucets.

OPPOSITE: The master bedroom is a mélange of patterns, colors, and furniture styles. A Bob Wilheit contemporary cherrywood tester bed is covered with an Indian wool shawl and stands in front of a wall painted a deep burnt orange.

ABOVE: A Roy Dowell painting hangs above a maple, ebony, and aluminum desk by artist Bob Wilheit. The table sports an assemblage of hand tools—including a pair of brass knuckles—and reflects Domergue's eclectic taste.

OPPOSITE: New French doors open onto a small deck overgrown with vines and a teak-root Indonesian bench.

Dojo Loft

KENSHO FURUYA

Visitors to aikido master Kensho Furuya's loft are surrounded by old Japan. Tatami-matted floors, walls hung with antique scrolls, and samurai swords breathe the sweet, herbaceous aroma of sandalwood incense. Hand-painted shoji screens enclose small alcoves where carved cabinets hold bronze figurines, celadon lions, and strikingly bold Oribe ceramics.

Remodeled in the style of a sixteenth-century shoin-zukuri, or warrior's residence, the 3,000-square-foot space with 45-foot ceilings was built in the early 1900s as a postal depository and later converted to a sugar warehouse. The single-story, block-long building, set back from the street, is now divided into 10 lofts. Rails embedded in the narrow asphalt parking lot recall the trains that once hauled in mail and sacks of sugar.

Furuya moved into the enclave near the downtown Arts District and Little Tokyo in 1984. "It's both home and dojo, or school," he explains. "I wanted a quiet, secluded space where my students could practice as well as a place to live. In olden days, the master taught seven days a week and lived in the dojo with his students."

Furuya's residence and school have evolved over the last 20 years. "I did this all myself—handpicked every piece of wood and nailed it in," he says. Such architectural remnants as antique doors and windows found in Japan have been incorporated into the loft, along with Japanese furnishings—chests, screens, pottery, and scrolls—collected over a lifetime by the Harvard- and University of Southern California–educated Zen priest, martial arts teacher, and author.

Originally, the space was one large room with a makeshift mezzanine and bathroom. There was no kitchen. Furuya decided to use the ground floor as his dojo and the upstairs for his living quarters. He divided the back of the first-floor room into a series of small alcoves: an elevated platform where visitors are entertained, a meditation room that doubles as a tearoom, and in the corner, a *mizuya*, in which the master prepares utensils for tea ceremonies.

The remaining space is open, laid with an elevated pine floor covered with mats where his students practice aikido. Each day after practice students of this non-combative martial art respectfully wipe the pine floor with wet towels. The resultant patina glows like a polished antique chest.

While the ground floor of Furuya's loft evokes ancient Japan, the narrow, crowded upstairs mezzanine is like a contemporary Tokyo apartment. Furuya added a kitchen along the back wall. A small storage area occupies the end of the mezzanine, adjacent to the bath. A large recliner in the middle of the room next to his kitchen table serves as command central. Here he works on his computer, watches TV, listens to music, and reads. "I have everything I need in one room," he says, "with most of it at arm's length."

The high ceiling allowed for a third-floor landing: a small storage room and a traditional Japanese bedroom that cantilevers over the studio below. Visitors from Japan are awed by the loft, says Furuya. "Everything is so Western in Japan today. They often tell me my dojo is more Japanese than those in Japan."

ABOVE: Aikido students perform noncombative martial arts movements.

OPPOSITE, TOP: Furuya created a traditional Japanese-style bedroom with a *tokonoma*, or alcove. The scroll in the alcove is changed seasonally or to welcome a visitor. An antique Japanese window adds to the room's traditional decor.

OPPOSITE, BOTTOM: Furuya's upstairs living quarters resembles a contemporary Tokyo apartment.

PAGE 58: A slightly elevated platform to the right of the stairs is where Furuya entertains guests of honor.

PAGE 59: Furuya's block-long building from the early 1900s once housed a postal depository and, later, a sugar warehouse.

ZEN GARDEN

Furuya created a tranquil Japanese garden on a train platform outside his loft as a transition between the bustling world outside and the peace he sought within. He enclosed his garden with a 200-year-old Japanese warehouse door and a 6-foot-high wooden slat-and-trellis wall. Bamboo pokes through the open trellis, which lights the garden and allows air to circulate. The inner entrance to the garden is through a tea-garden gate typical of those found in Japanese scholars' retreats. Two-foot-high redwood planters on either side of the path hold Heavenly Bamboo (*Nandina*) that shades and cools. Asian begonias and Yesterday, Today, and Tomorrow flowers (*Brunfelsia*) grow in pots along a narrow path. Flanked by a symbolic stream of river stones, the loose-set pavers give way underfoot, making soft crunching sounds. "An old samurai tradition that allowed them to hear if anyone approached," Furuya explains. "It's a natural burglar alarm."

RIGHT, TOP: A 200-year-old Japanese warehouse gate chosen for its size and strength as well as its symbolism makes a majestic entry for Furuya's warehouse loft and school. The gate's open wire–lattice top allows for air to circulate and helps keep his garden cool.

RIGHT, BOTTOM: The garden is washed down each day by senior students. The wet stones and bamboo give arriving students a sense of the refreshing, clean air just after a rain. Japanese script on four pavers next to the walk spell out the characters for peace, happiness, long life, and prosperity.

OPPOSITE: A tea-garden gate typical of scholars' retreats in Japan marks the inner entrance to a small bamboo garden. Japanese calligraphy on the gate spells out Furuya's poetic name, Bansetsu-An, "Retreat of the Unskilled One."

ABOVE: A colorful suit of Japanese armor seems to stand guard at the base of the stairs leading to the mezzanine living quarters. Alongside the armor are antique scrolls, Oribe pottery, a large storage vase, and a celadon lion.

OPPOSITE: A black lacquer and gold-leaf shrine from Japan houses memorial tablets of Furuya's teacher and parents. The room is used both for meditation and formal Japanese tea ceremonies.

Eurostyle Modern

VELVET HAMMERSCHMIDT & MARK FRIEDMAN

Transplanted New Yorker Mark Friedman, a software CEO, always wanted to live in a loft. He didn't realize his dream, however, until moving from his tiny Manhattan apartment to a spacious abode in Santa Monica. He and his wife, interior designer Velvet Hammerschmidt, now live in a penthouse loft with 15-foot-tall ceilings. Friedman says happily, "We're within walking distance of the Third Street Promenade, Montana Avenue, the ocean, and both our offices."

Living close to both work and the ocean always was Friedman's dream, but its realization was difficult. "There weren't any big, spacious loft buildings in Santa Monica," he says. "They didn't exist."

He solved the problem by making building partners of five like-minded friends. Architect Bill Brantley of Aarts in Santa Monica designed the three-story, six-unit building, a complex of corner lofts with parchment-painted corrugated-metal siding, in the seaside community's Broadway Commercial District.

Each partner took one of the approximately 1,800-square-foot lofts to live in or resell. In the four-plus years it took to complete, Friedman became engaged to Hammerschmidt. "What looked like a decent-size unit for a single guy," he says, "suddenly looked cramped."

He bought a friend's loft next door and combined the two into one 3,800-square-foot space. The loft is divided into two separate suites with a long gallery corridor between, accessed by a private elevator. On one side are the open-plan kitchen, dining room, and "maid's room." The opposite wing holds their living room, office/library, and powder room. A bedroom and bath, on a raised level reached by way of painted steel stairs, anchor each end of the loft.

The most distinctive architectural aspect of the space is the 9-degree-canted south-facing wall that runs the length of the building. Living room and dining room spaces punch through the exterior wall and cantilever over the two floors below. Fourteen floor-to-ceiling windows flood the rooms with light. Giant X's—steel seismic braces—punctuate the walls in the hallway and bedrooms.

Designer Hammerschmidt's primary goal was to imbue the space with the feeling of "home." She also wanted a warmed-up modern decor. Instead of cold concrete floors, she installed Douglas fir set on end for texture. She stained the floor and other woodwork espresso brown. The kitchen floor is whitewashed. Like an area rug, she explains, it helps define the space. Frequently barefoot, Hammerschmidt chose to cover the bedroom and library floors in looped wool carpet for comfort.

For the furniture, Hammerschmidt selected modern Eurostyle furnishings—a B&B Italia sofa, Driade tables, Philippe Starck dining chairs, and Fontana Arte globes—and a few midcentury pieces. Upholstery is covered in luxurious materials: silk velvets, Ultrasuede, and leather, in a subtle, sophisticated palette of gray, black, and coffee.

A state-of-the-art AMX home automation system controls lighting, temperature, window shades, and entertainment center. Just as she'd hoped, says Hammerschmidt, "The loft has all the comforts of a real home."

ABOVE: An avid cook, Hammerschmidt installed a sleek, Bulthaup kitchen with a stainless-steel backsplash and oak cabinets finished with a dark stain. A large center island covered with Carrara marble with a trio of Knoll Studio bar stools is a gathering place for friends. Stainless-steel appliance garages at one end keep the kitchen neat and tidy. Adjacent to the garages, a customized door resembling a cabinet leads to a small "maid's room" that Hammerschmidt uses for her design library.

RIGHT: Philippe Starck Olly Tango bent plywood-and-chrome chairs surround the dining table Hammerschmidt fashioned out of a wine riddler's rack.

OPPOSITE, TOP: A private elevator brings the couple onto a gallery corridor that connects the two former units. Recessed blue LED lights along the floor and a trio of hanging orange globes above create a dramatic entry.

OPPOSITE, BOTTOM: The couple's loft features an open-plan dining room and kitchen area. A Louis Poulsen Artichoke chandelier hangs elegantly over the dining table.

PAGE 66: The couple's living room is appointed with sleek Eurostyle furnishings. A stairway leads to the master bedroom suite and a roof-deck terrace.

PAGE 67: Architect Bill Brantley of Aarts designed the three-story loft complex in Santa Monica's Broadway Commercial District.

SMART HOUSE LOFT

Hammerschmidt and Friedman made their house truly smart by running an array of Category 5 cable, speaker, and video wires throughout the walls. All lighting, temperature, window shades, and entertainment systems are controlled by an AMX home automation system with a Pronto control. Coming home after work, a push of the "I'm home" button dims the lights and plays soothing classical music. When they leave, pushing a button shuts everything off and closes the shades. The shades also are programmed to raise and lower throughout the day, controlling light, protecting furnishings, and ensuring privacy. "We have fourteen windows," says Friedman. "If we had to raise and lower each of them, we'd go crazy." In addition, entertainment systems are connected: the couple can record a program in the living room and finish watching it in the bedroom. Similarly, music selections can run throughout the loft or be controlled individually by control pads in each room. And if there's a power outage? Friedman quips: "We'll get out the candles."

A large sculpture made from an old textile turbine stands next to the window in the dining area.

ABOVE: A large structural-steel cross adds architectural interest to the guest bedroom. A leather-framed mirror leans against the wall to make the room appear larger.

LEFT: The living room features a comfortable B&B Italia sectional sofa and a leather ottoman/coffee table.

ABOVE: The limestone-clad bathroom features a pair of Agape sinks mounted on top of the counter. A pair of his-and-her walk-in closets sandwich the tub.

LEFT: The master bedroom overlooks the living room and study below. The steel stairs outside lead to a large upstairs deck the couple use as an outdoor entertaining room.

OPPOSITE: The couple's home office stands on an elevated platform and overlooks the living room. Built-in bookcases and storage fit under the stairs and partially wrap the back wall.

Test Garage

ROZ HAYES & DANI STOLLER

Furniture designers Roz Hayes and Dani Stoller's loft serves as warehouse, furniture showroom, test lab, and home. A former 1920s garage for First Edison Company service trucks, the one-story building is five minutes east of Chinatown, near the Los Angeles train switching yards. Hayes calls the 2,800-square-foot space under a lofty 28-foot-tall ceiling their "giant play box."

"To design, you have to put yourself in a child-like place in your head," Hayes explains. "Playful objects in a lofty setting inspire us." This explains the Pop Art baby bottle, 6-foot-tall toothbrush, and enormous foam foot. Combined with the couple's theatrical furnishings—a Plexiglas cocktail table filled with fake roses; an electric blue, womblike sofa wired for stereo—they embody their Lush Life company's philosophy of "laughing, loving, and luscious living."

The pair sought a place in which they could both live and work. When they found this building, they realized the storefront windows along the brick building's facade could highlight an ideal home showroom. An adjacent roll-up garage door, offering easy access for their oversized furnishings, sold them.

The place, they discovered, did have a downside: while the mezzanine had a makeshift kitchen and bathroom, downstairs there was no heating or plumbing. In a creative solution to the plumbing problem, Stoller installed a high-pressure pump that hooked into the upstairs line, allowing them to install a kitchen downstairs at the rear of the loft, as well as a bathroom under the stairs.

The couple furnished the new kitchen with cabinets purchased at a local home salvage yard and a 30-foot-long upholstered bar they had designed for a Beverly Hills nightclub. The open space in front of the kitchen is dedicated to their revolving warehouse of furniture, pieces sought after for music videos, television commercials, clubs, and restaurants.

Although they initially used the large space for furniture making, they have since rented another loft nearby as a workshop. "The live/work idea was initially what attracted us," Hayes says, "but the reality of the grinding dust and paint fumes wasn't so great. It was a mess a lot of the time and didn't feel much like a home."

To make the loft feel more homey and to warm up the unheated space, they laid slate blue wall-to-wall carpet in the main loft space and a light industrial carpet in the adjacent showroom. A small office under a low corrugated ceiling between the kitchen and stairs is illuminated by hospital operating-room lamps. Hayes explains: "It was less drafty away from the windows."

A vintage Andy Warhol cow poster presides over the mezzanine landing, where a large storage closet has replaced the top-of-the-stairs kitchenette. The existing bathroom and enclosed storage room now serve as a guest bedroom suite.

For their master bedroom site, the pair took the front of the building, underneath the exposed vaulted ceiling. An elaborate carved headboard stands against an old brick wall. To brighten the space, Hayes stenciled bold black flowers on a white floor, then hung fuchsia-colored, plastic drapery over the windows. "They cut down on drafts, yet allow light to pass through," explains Hayes. "There's no heating in this old building and it gets pretty chilly in here. It's hard to be creative when you're cold."

LEFT: A 30-foot-long bar shaped like an airplane wing, originally designed for a Beverly Hills nightclub, serves as the couple's kitchen counter.

OPPOSITE: The couple placed their home furniture showroom in the front of the loft, near the shop-front windows.

PAGE 76: A large roll-up garage door was one of the selling points for the owners, whose large-scale furnishings easily fit through the door. Industrial windows bring in plenty of light but also make the unheated space cold and drafty in winter.

PAGE 77: The one-story brick building once served as a garage for the First Edison Company service trucks.

LEFT: For a bit of sparkle, in a small window overlooking the loft, Hayes hung crystals she was saving to make a chandelier with. A golden Pucci mannequin by Ruben Toledo and a pair of vintage Venetian hanging glass lamps decorate the bedroom corner.

OPPOSITE: A vintage Andy Warhol cow poster presides over the mezzanine landing, where an enclosed storage room now serves as a guest bedroom.

BELOW: An ornate headboard flanked by a pair of '70s serpentine floor lamps stands against the exposed brick wall. Hayes's stenciled floral floor, fuchsia-colored furnishings, and plastic drapery reflect her strong personal style.

FLOWER POWER

Adding a dramatic touch to her master bedroom, Hayes warmed up her cold concrete floor with bold, black flowers inspired by the plumeria tree in her garden. On thin cardboard, she drew six stylized flowers ranging from 6 to 13 inches in diameter, then cut out the designs to create a stencil for each flower. Before applying the pattern, she painted the floor with white epoxy so the black contrast color would adhere evenly to the surface. Beginning in one corner and working from the outside in, she used a pencil to outline each bloom in the design she wanted on the floor, then inked the outline with a black pen. Painting over the stencil sometimes resulted in paint running under the cardboard and ruining the design. As a result, she often just removed the stencil after outlining the form and handpainted between the lines. Vines connecting the flowers were done freehand. A clear polyurethane topcoat protects the floor.

ABOVE: The small office features their tilted bookcase and Duces Wild sofa. A pair of operating-room lamps lights the space located next to the kitchen.

OPPOSITE: After plumbing the downstairs, they added a small bathroom under the stairs. Leftover red plywood panels and a giant Pop Art–style toothbrush decorate the bathroom. A metal toilet-paper holder they fashioned displays multiple rolls, while a small plywood cabinet adjacent to the toilet hides the plumbing.

Working Castle

GOTTFRIED & RENATE HELNWEIN

Austrian multimedia artist Gottfried Helnwein lives half the year in an Irish castle surrounded by woods and lowing herds and the other half in a loft catty-corner from Crazy Gideon's wholesale appliances. Nary a tree or cow populates the bleak urban spaces south of Alameda Street; only abandoned shopping carts, feral cats, and architecture students from SCI-Arc color the landscape. "Living in Ireland is the exact opposite of Los Angeles," Helnwein says. "There is an anonymity and freedom here to do as you please that inspires me. I need both places for my work."

Helnwein's wife, Renate, found the perfect live-work environment for them in two separate but tangent buildings on Traction Avenue, now the main thoroughfare of Los Angeles' Arts District. The living-quarters loft occupies the top floor of a three-story brick coffee-and-tea warehouse built in

1918. The ground floor now houses a coffee shop. The 2,300-square-foot loft was open space when the Helnweins first saw it, except for a small built-in kitchen and bathroom. Large windows at one end, brick walls, exposed ceiling joists, aluminum ducts, and raw-wood columns remain from the loft's original interior elements. At the back of the loft, away from the windows, they added two bedrooms.

Gottfried's 4,300-square-foot painting studio is in the adjacent single-story brick building. This space, with an 18-foot ceiling, has functioned as a bakery, seaweed warehouse, and truck depot. It was already divided into two equal parts when the Helnweins leased it, a narrow hallway lined with industrial windows connecting the two spaces. Helnwein hangs his finished works in the front studio and uses the back one for painting. A stairway in the painting studio leads to a mezzanine, which serves as their son's bedroom and as a storage area; an office is tucked underneath. Needing more wall space for canvases up to 30 feet wide, the couple built a freestanding L-shaped wall, attaching steel straps to exposed girders for stability. Their large collection of art books and catalogs fills a table crafted from salvaged wood and a wall of built-in bookcases.

Furnishings in their Traction Avenue loft are casual and eclectic: a Chinese daybed and bench, a Moroccan table, American office chairs around a Craftsman dining table, a couple of contemporary couches. A vintage American stove Renate found and installed in the kitchen adds personality to the simple, utilitarian space. "It's so easy to fix up a loft. There's nothing to finish," Renate says. "You can do whatever you want—put walls up, pull them down, move things around. Then you just buy a few pieces of furniture and move in. It's so much simper than restoring a castle."

ABOVE: Gottfried has a one-minute commute to his art studio located on the first floor of the adjacent building. One of his new 30-foot-long canvases of the Mohave Desert hangs along the brick wall of the building. A preexisting mezzanine became a bedroom and storage area; Gottfried's office space is nestled below the staircase.

OPPOSITE: The Helnweins' built-in bookcases hold their large collection of art books and catalogs.

PAGE 84: Gottfried's back studio, which has functioned as a bakery, seaweed warehouse, and truck depot, now displays his giant canvases.

PAGE 85: The 1918 brick building was initially used as a coffee-and-tea warehouse. Today the first floor is a coffeehouse and local gathering spot for the community of artists and architecture students from the nearby Southern California Institute of Architecture.

OLD-FASHIONED CHARM

As in many no-frills lofts, the Helnweins' kitchen was bare-bones: two parallel rows of simple, blond cabinets topped with a concrete counter. There were no appliances. Renate had her heart set on a vintage American stove. "I wanted a gas stove," she says, "and good aesthetics were very important to me." An artist friend helped her find the perfect solution at the A-1 Stove Hospital in Los Angeles: an early '50s Wedgwood. The model had an oven and broiler, a chrome stove top with four gas burners and a griddle, a clock, and a timer. It looked brand new. An added attraction: a cooking chart on the inside of the oven door spells out temperature and cooking times for cakes, cookies, and roasts. "The stove adds real personality to the kitchen," says Renate, "and it's wonderful to cook on. I love it."

ABOVE: A '50s Wedgwood stove adds personality to the kitchen.

LEFT: The Helnweins enclosed two bedrooms near the front of the loft and left the remainder of the space open. Their Craftsman dining table is surrounded by an array of vintage chairs.

PREVIOUS SPREAD: A stairway in the Helnweins' painting studio leads to a mezzanine, which serves as their son's bedroom and a storage area; an office is tucked underneath. The painting is Gottfried's *Head of a Child*.

ABOVE: A daybed stationed by the loft's front windows and blanketed with pillows makes a comfy place to sit and read.

OPPOSITE: Helnwein's paintings of Native American Indian chiefs line the living room's exposed brick wall.

Modern Romance

LAURA HULL

In 1996, artist Laura Hull was living across from the beach in a two-bedroom mobile home in a Carlsbad trailer park. Now, the fine arts photographer and *Metropolitan Home* magazine editor is light-years away: loft-living Los Angeles in a 1940s building that once was a terry-cloth bathrobe factory.

"I felt I was working too much and not doing enough art at the time," says Hull, explaining her move to the Santa Fe Art Colony in Los Angeles, an artist community set in former toy and clothing workshops.

Hull's first task after moving into the one-story brick building was anything but artistic. Refinishing the concrete floors, which a previous tenant had splattered with paint, took two weeks of stripping, sealing, and polishing.

Next came reclaiming the mezzanine areas in each of the 1,300-square-foot loft's two large rooms.

Electrical lines and gas pipes ran at mid-thigh height through the center of each space, essentially making them useful only for storage. By rerouting the utility lines and pipes along the ceiling, she turned the front room's small space above the open-plan kitchen and living room area into a small library; the mezzanine above her back studio became her bedroom.

To access the small library, she added a wooden staircase salvaged from a neighbor's loft. A cabinet she built under the stairs serves as a combined storage area and pantry for the kitchen on the opposite wall.

Originally the kitchen held a sink and a single cabinet. A vintage O'Keefe & Merritt stove stood on an adjacent wall. Hull added a row of top and bottom cabinets and rerouted the gas line so the stove could be placed along the new galley kitchen wall. She sprayed unfinished discount retail cabinets with multiple layers of matte-white lacquer and achieved a slick, modern look with nickel-plated hardware.

Although she painted the loft walls in a tailored Swiss coffee color, Hull purposely left the peeling, weathered paint on the ceiling and overhead beams to recall the building's age. She explains: "I like to see the contrast of textures."

Hull chose contemporary furnishings in blond woods and employed tactile fabrics—Ultrasuede, mohair, sea grass—to heighten the contrasts. Underfoot, flokati and sisal area rugs add warmth to the scoured concrete floors; artwork from colony friends and the artist's own photographs enliven the walls. "It's great to be in an artist environment, to exchange work and keep an artistic dialogue going in my life," Hull says.

After completing the inside of her home, Hull turned her attention to the dirt corridor between the two buildings at the loft's back entrance. The once-drab space is now a small oasis planted with hydrangeas, cacti, and fig trees. Hummingbirds like to nest in the needle cactus and turtledoves roost in the bougainvillea trellis behind the patio table. "People are always surprised how quiet it is here," Hull says. "I do occasionally hear muffled traffic noises, but mostly I hear the cooing of the doves. It's a great environment to create art."

LEFT: Hull created a new galley kitchen with cabinets from a discount retail store and a vintage stove.

OPPOSITE: Hull added a small library/meditation room in the front mezzanine. An old wrought-iron gate and a paper sculpture made by an artist friend function as see-through screens.

PAGE 94: A flokati area rug adds warmth to the scoured concrete floor in the living room. Artwork from colony friends enlivens the walls. The staircase leads to a small library.

PAGE 95: The Santa Fe Art Colony, established in 1987, is one of L.A.'s first loft-living artists' complexes. It comprises three residential buildings with 57 studios and between 60 and 70 artists; a fourth building on the premises is a sponge manufacturing company.

PRACTICAL DREAMLAND

With the ambience of her loft a bit cold, Hull says, she wanted her bedroom to have some softness to it. She began by hanging premade linen panels on unfinished wood knobs hot-glued onto a beam along the back wall. She scraped peeling paint from the weathered beams, and liked the resulting patina so much she left it at that. A low-slung commercial light fixture is hung upside down, four feet below the ceiling. The white fluorescent light bounces off the milk-white ceiling, creating a soft reflected glow in the bedroom and studio below. The romantic pièce de résistance is a mosquito net hanging from a small metal canopy attached to the ceiling. In most seasons, the white netting is flipped over sprinkler pipes. Come summer, with no window screens and a proliferation of mosquitoes, Hull gladly sleeps under it. "It's very practical," she says, "as well as romantic."

ABOVE: Hull's mosquito netting–draped bed located in the back mezzanine overlooks her office.

LEFT: Hull painted the walls white but left the ceiling and beams in their original weathered condition for texture.

OPPOSITE: Hull uses the loft's back room for her office and bedroom. She installed a darkroom behind the built-in bookcase and the front living quarters.

ABOVE: An oasis in the corridor between two buildings at the rear of the loft is a favorite "quiet spot."

ABOVE, LEFT: Hull uses the loft's back room for her office and bedroom. Large factory windows flood the space with natural light.

OPPOSITE: Hull fitted a raffia-like fabric top to the table she fashioned out of a door. Low maple chairs were custom-designed by a Los Angeles artist; her own photograph hangs above.

L.A. Bohème

ELIZABETH KRAMER & ROBERT HELLER

Realtor Robert Heller and fashion designer Elizabeth Kramer fell under the spell of a picturesque brick building on Vignes Street, built in 1911, that once housed a bakery. No wonder. Overgrown with bougainvillea, climbing roses, and jasmine, the four-story building once redolent of yeasty dough now breathes a fresh, urban-romantic charm.

Faintly visible on the building's side is a sign advertising the late Los Angeles Baking Company. From the rooftop garden, the view to the northwest is of city skyline and Frank Gehry's Disney Hall; to the north, the blue-gray backdrop of the San Gabriel Mountains; and to the east, Boyle Heights. A hundred feet from the building's back alley, the First Street Bridge spans the Los Angeles River.

The couple shares the second floor of the old bakery with their two sheepdogs, Wadsworth and Wellington. Through an open window, they eavesdrop on the conversations of passersby. "It reminds me of Paris," says Heller, who lived in France on and off for over two decades. "It's a real neighborhood. People walk their dogs, meet neighbors on the street, take time to talk."

Since both Kramer and Heller are Francophiles, it is fitting that their loft resembles a bohemian Les Halles apartment. The decor includes vintage chandeliers, Grecian statuary, and a mélange of flea market furnishings in exotic animal fabrics. Store mannequins wear Kramer's fashions and her collection of vintage dresses. A stuffed toy orangutan hangs from a conduit in the living room. "We love to hear people's comments," Kramer says, "when they suddenly spy Ophelia."

Guests rhapsodize about the dramatic, low-slung arches and 9-foot-high concrete ceiling. "You can still see the grain marks from the wood framing from when they poured the ceiling and then removed the boards," Heller says. The couple left the ceiling off-white and painted the concrete floor and walls in terra-cotta red.

Kramer's studio and a small library are near the entrance of the 1,470-square-foot open-plan loft. A working cupid water fountain stands in between the two spaces, surrounded by a moveable wire garden fence. "It keeps the dogs from using it as a bathtub," Kramer explains. A kitchen with a center island, vintage General Electric stove, and new commercial refrigerator stands across from the living room in the center of the loft. Next to the front window, the single light source for the room, a table provides a place to read and work. In the corner is the couple's bedroom, festooned in silk fabrics with Chinese dragons and bold stripes and embellished with scads of pillows.

In keeping with the Franco-bohemian theme, the walls are blanketed with an array of watercolors, oils, and sketches of Parisian life: cafes, churches, bridges, and people. Heller paid only 20 francs for the entire collection—the contents of a locked leather satchel he found at a flea market and remembers as "the best grab bag of my life."

The realtor, who once lived in a 10,000-square-foot former home of Howard Hughes close by the eighth green of the Wilshire Country Club, never dreamed he would live in a downtown loft. "I'm happier here than anywhere I've ever been," he says. "And I've finally found the right place for the art."

ABOVE: A fountain the couple salvaged from a San Fernando home stands between the library and Kramer's studio. Before they set up a small moveable fence around it, their sheepdogs used it as a giant dog bowl and upon occasion, a bathtub.

OPPOSITE, TOP: To the right of the entry, the designer tucked her studio under one of the arches. Mannequins throughout the loft sport her fashions and accessories.

OPPOSITE, BOTTOM: The couple added a green marble top to the existing center island and installed a new commercial refrigerator along the wall. The concrete ceiling still bears the wood-framing marks from its pouring.

PAGE 102: The couple built in floor-to-ceiling bookcases along their library wall opposite Kramer's studio. A vintage flea market chandelier hangs overhead.

PAGE 103: The 1911 building, once the Los Angeles Baking Company, is now overgrown with bougainvillea, climbing roses, and jasmine.

BOHEMIAN BOUDOIR

Kramer placed a queen-size box spring and mattress in the back corner of the loft and went to work with fabrics selected to create a romantic, tentlike ambience. She festooned two panels of yellow-and-gold-striped silk on the ceiling. Hemmed at each end, the fabric panels are attached to 6-foot-long extension rods resting in hooks above the bed. Below, an angel-motif blanket with tassels covers the box spring. On the top of the bed are a green brocade down comforter and pillows covered in vintage fabrics. Red-and-gold dragon fabric panels hand-tacked onto a conduit drape the bedside to complete the Scheherazade look. Joint compound spread on the walls with a spackling knife furthers the Old World, cracked-plaster appearance. Surrounded by walls painted a flattering blush pink and hung with a half dozen of her favorite paintings, Kramer says she feels "luxuriously cocooned in my own private art gallery."

ABOVE: A round table by the window serves as a place to read and work. They purchased the hand-painted French commode in the bathroom at the Pasadena Flea Market.

RIGHT: The couple's fabric-enclosed bedroom offers a romantic retreat.

ABOVE: A faux-leopard covered chair, a colorful Japanese kimono, and lots of artwork enhance the couple's bare-bones bathroom.

OPPOSITE: Orangutan Ophelia, the loft mascot, hangs over the living room, the focal point of which is a Chinese cabinet surrounded by vintage furnishings. Parisian artwork on the walls is from a single lucky "grab bag" flea-market find of Heller's.

Department Store on Broadway

DORIAN LaPADURA & FRAN VINCENT

Twentieth-century design cognoscente Dorian LaPadura has lived in architectural gems by Frank Lloyd Wright, Frank Gehry, and Gregory Ain since selling his mural business in 1995 and moving west from New York City. He was feeling the itch to move again in the late '90s when a friend told him about a loft with lots of space, reasonable rent, and an intriguing location.

When he saw the 1919 five-story Kress Building on Broadway in the Historic Theater District, LaPadura was as excited by the neighborhood as by the space. His fourth-floor loft, shared with Museum of Contemporary Art store manager Fran Vincent, overlooks the 1911 Orpheum Theater (now the Palace) and directly abuts the 1931 Los Angeles Theater. Iconic Clifton's Cafeteria, also established in 1931, is across the street. St. Vincent's Court, a colorful back alley lined with ethnic restaurants, marks the entrance to the loft. In the 1950s, when Bullock's department store owned the property, this mini Covent Garden was an outdoor flower market.

LaPadura's first few weeks in the loft were more nitty-gritty. On hands and knees, he stripped the hardwood floors of imbedded encaustic paint, a waxlike pigment left from the previous artist-tenant. He spackled more than 100 holes in the ceiling where retail space partitions had been anchored into concrete slabs. He replastered columns that had cracked and separated from the floor. Three coats of plaster and white paint later, the loft has a pristine, gallerylike appearance.

The long, narrow space with windows only at one end posed a significant design challenge. "I wanted to avoid the claustrophobic feeling that adding walls would create," he says, "and I needed to bring as much light into the space as possible." To that end, LaPadura, a fine artist and design consultant, added three orbit mirrors along the south wall. The rotating mirrors reflect light back into the space; overhead, a row of track lights runs the length of the room. An up light illuminates the ceiling in the dining room and kitchen at the rear of the loft; other task lamps light the rest.

In a subtle move to maintain the open feeling, LaPadura divided the loft into four distinct zones, taking his cue from the dramatic fluted columns that punctuated the space. The layout permits an uninterrupted visual flow, in which pieces of furniture define and mark the boundaries of the living areas. A desk adjacent to a large exposed column juts horizontally to divide his paint studio from the living room. The bedroom is sandwiched between the living room sofa and a low bookcase. The kitchen is tucked behind the bookcase. He kept the corner L-alcove for his painting gallery. There he stores materials in plastic containers on wheels, "so I can move everything out in fifteen minutes when I want to work on a large canvas." Furnishings are a mix of twentieth-century masters—Le Corbusier, Charles Eames, Alvar Alto—along with the designer's own modern pieces.

LaPadura admits that an urban loft is a long way from a home with a famous pedigree. "In the Wright house I was constantly aware of nature. A snowfall, squirrels in the trees would distract me," he says. "When you're trying to paint and create you don't want diversions."

ABOVE: LaPadura stripped the hardwood floors of embedded encaustic paint and spackled more than a hundred holes in the ceiling where retail space partitions had been anchored into concrete slabs.

OPPOSITE, TOP: LaPadura stores paint supplies and camping equipment in Metro Wire shelving carts and plastic containers with lids from a discount retail store.

OPPOSITE, BOTTOM: A large mirror opposite the kitchen helps enlarge the narrow loft space.

PAGE 110: A Charles Eames Eiffel Tower chair pulls up to LaPadura's dining table; sleek contemporary cabinets line the wall.

PAGE 111: The five-story Kress Building's beige facade features horizontal bands of pivot windows.

LaPadura painted the L-shaped room a warm white to bounce the light around and make the loft seem as light and airy as possible. He added a jolt of complementary color at either end: cool purple by the windows, orange in the kitchen.

ABOVE, TOP: LaPadura hangs his paintings along the north wall of the loft. All the walls are painted a gallery white to showcase art and furnishings.

ABOVE, BOTTOM: A modern bench marks the entry to LaPadura's loft.

OPPOSITE: Screens protect art materials from direct sunlight and baffle noise from Broadway traffic—"the busiest street in downtown," says LaPadura.

Urban Oasis

DAVID MOCARSKI

Rumbling trains may rattle windows and vibrate the ground like a mild earthquake, but that doesn't discourage artist and furniture designer David Mocarski from living at the Brewery. Lured by the prospect of living in an artists' community and having ample space to work in, he has had five different lofts in the rambling complex over the last two decades. Situated on a 20-acre parcel of land off North Main Street, directly behind the Los Angeles train switching yards, most of the twenty-one buildings from the late '30s and early '40s were once the property of the Eastside Brewery and Edison Electric.

When a former warehouse next door to his previous loft became available, he decided to take over the more secluded back corner of the building. The space itself was smaller, but it featured an enclosed yard, which he coveted. "I wanted to be able to have friends over for barbecues," he says. "This is California after all." In addition, he liked the large industrial garage door, which slides up and opens his workshop to the lush, green garden.

The first time Mocarski saw the inside of the red brick building that was to be his loft, it was a large open area with a 24-foot-high vaulted ceiling and a grid of factory windows on one wall. To make the place livable, he first sandblasted the space to remove years of grit, then sheet-rocked the ceiling for insulation. Because of the height, he was able to add a steel-and-concrete second level within the space, thereby doubling the square footage. He decided to reserve downstairs for his studio, where he makes furniture prototypes for Arkkit Forms, his residential and commercial furnishings company, and use the upstairs for living.

Today, the sophisticated mezzaninelike level beneath exposed-steel trusses is filled with his modern furniture and art. Guests enter up a new steel staircase from the workshop below into an open-plan living and dining room with an enclosed kitchen and bath nestled in the corner. A pair of original skylights and a band of old factory windows along the southeast wall bring light into the interior. Additional up lights attached to overhead beams reflect off the white vaulted ceiling to create a soft, tranquil environment. "It's a diffused source of illumination," he says, "much like a city light on a foggy night."

Mocarski halved the living quarters with an 8-foot-tall partition down the center of the room, using one side as a home office and studio. Students from Pasadena's Art Center College of Design, where he teaches environmental design, often gather around the long worktable. A bay of tall, sleek cabinets he devised house various projects and papers. In the top corner of the end cabinet he added a stylish, built-in birdcage for his pet finches.

Although Mocarski is an avid traveler and has always loved the romance of trains, living 30 feet from the noisy Los Angeles switching yards posed a serious challenge. He located the master bedroom behind the office as far from the windows and train yard as possible, then hung a linen curtain along the wall behind his bed to help muffle sounds. Insulated birch panels completely cover the loft's front and back brick walls for soundproofing. They also give the space a more finished look. A grid of drafty factory windows has been replaced with new aluminum casement sliders, which add yet another layer of insulation.

Outside, Mocarski transformed his asphalt yard into an urban oasis. He dug a deep trough at the perimeter and planted green-timber bamboo, poplar, and mulberry trees to create a cooler, quieter garden environment as well as an intimate place to entertain friends. "The quality of light coming through the trees is lovely," he says. And when a train passes by on the track next to his yard while he's entertaining? "We stop talking for a moment until it passes. It's part of the equation of living in an industrial area."

ABOVE: Across from the dining room, Mocarski fashioned an enclosed kitchen of black and white laminate and bird's-eye maple cabinets made from existing materials in his downstairs workshop.

OPPOSITE, TOP: Mocarski planted fast-growing bamboo to help baffle noise from the nearby train yard as well as to introduce some greenery to the industrial area.

OPPOSITE, BOTTOM: Mocarski designed the sleek polished aluminum and woven contrast-fabric chairs and the dining table topped with salt-and-pepper granite.

PAGE 118: Mocarski added a wall to divide the upstairs space into two equal zones. Reaching just below the trusses, the wall maintains the airy, open loft feel. A Scandinavian-modern, steel and cast concrete stove heats the entire loft. A pair of existing skylights bring diffused light into the interior he painted a cool, celadon green.

PAGE 119: A roll-up industrial garage door leads to Mocarski's downstairs workshop/garage in the former maintenance warehouse at the Brewery.

THE BEAUTY OF BUILT-INS

Wanting to display his small collectibles—toy cars, Japanese robots, and contemporary Venetian porcelains—to their best advantage, Mocarski built a plywood shelf resembling a long light box nearly the width of his studio. The light comes from a trio of fluorescent tubes inside the box; a milk-white sheet of Plexiglas is set flush with the top. The illuminated shelf shows off the small objects in their best light. Nearby, a 16-foot-long bay of birch plywood cabinets neatly houses his class projects, files, and half a dozen guitar cases. To streamline further, he got rid of an old birdcage and built a new home for his two dozen pet finches at the end of the unit. A sliding shelf below facilitates cleaning. "Everyone has things they love and want to look at," Mocarski says. "The trick is to display them in a pleasing, organized environment."

ABOVE: Honduras mahogany bookshelves in Mocarski's studio abut his pet finches' cage.

LEFT: Mocarski replaced a grid of old puttied factory windows that rattled when the trains passed with screened aluminum casement sliders, which offer better insulation and ventilation. A narrow shadow box shows off his eclectic collections.

ABOVE: Mocarski designed birch cabinets for his bathroom, then painted the walls chocolate-maroon and chartreuse. A carved wood alligator and mask from Ghana decorate the space.

OPPOSITE: A birdcage incorporated into a corner of his built-in storage cabinets holds two dozen pet finches. The designer's aluminum and Plexiglas lighting fixtures illuminate his large worktable.

LEFT AND OPPOSITE: Mocarski's white linen curtain, hung on an aluminum bar with large grommets, baffles noise from the nearby train yard. He insulated the front and back walls of the loft with birch paneling.

Safe House

NANCY MONTGOMERY

A parade could pass by furniture designer Nancy Montgomery's first-floor Traction Avenue loft in Los Angeles and she wouldn't hear a thing: Sleeping in a walk-in vault with 14-inch-thick walls and a 200-pound steel door has its advantages. The building was constructed in 1917 for the Ben Hur Coffee & Spice Company, and the firm used the first floor as their business office. Their former vault is now Montgomery's bedroom. Other architectural remnants of the coffee company remain, including a giant scale in the basement and a big hole in the lobby where the spice grinder once stood.

Montgomery has had Reform, her commercial furniture company, in the five-story brick building—situated between Little Tokyo and the Los Angeles River in the center of the Arts District—since 1987. She was looking for a space to house her burgeoning furniture company in the late '80s when a leasing agent introduced her to the building surrounded by ethnic restaurants and art galleries, and with a quaint general store across the street. She fell in love with the front-corner loft boasting an oak-trimmed entry, 3-foot-wide columns, and large storefront windows.

Initially, she used the 4,000 square feet to fabricate her goods and serve as a showroom while she lived in a 1920s Spanish home in the Los Feliz hills. But as her business grew, she began manufacturing elsewhere. She decided to cut costs and her commute by turning the loft into her home and a small design office. Her goal: "I wanted it to feel like a home," she says, "not some big cavernous warehouse."

Beyond the entrance, through an oak vestibule that she filled with ferns, Montgomery segregated her business and living quarters by placing her office to the left of the vestibule and the living room to the right, maintaining the open-plan layout. Her bedroom is located between the two spaces toward the rear of the loft, softened and more homelike with wall-to-wall carpeting and grass cloth covering the walls. "Friends often think it's a bit strange to sleep in a safe," she says, "but it's actually very cozy."

In the corner of her living room, she built out an enclosed space where she once made furniture on her power saw; the space now serves as her dining room and library. She kept the walls lower than the 14-foot ceilings to maintain the loft's airy feel. Inside, she added floor-to-ceiling bookshelves on one wall and, in the corner, a built-in birch seating unit inspired by the early California modernists she admires. She painted the walls a "girlie" pastel pink. Outside, the walls are red, defining the exterior and adding a jolt of color in the otherwise gallery-white environment.

Directly behind the dining room, she gutted what was left of the tawdry Big Bang Café's kitchen, a restaurant which occupied the space in the '80s. A new kitchen of sleek birch cabinets with a recessed niche for flowers has taken its place. A wood grid set on the diagonal hovers over the kitchen as well as the corner sitting area "to lower the ceiling and create a more intimate, homelike space without closing off the room," she says. Adjacent to the kitchen, in tight, shiplike quarters, she added a bathroom, shower, utility room, and storage closets, tapping into the existing plumbing from the restaurant's former bathrooms and makeshift shower.

Montgomery says she occasionally thinks of her former home in the hills but finds living and working in the same space both convenient and inspiring. "If I wake up in the middle of the night with an idea, I can get up and work on it," she says. And, in a city infamous for its traffic, she has no commute.

ABOVE: The preexisting oak-trimmed entry and enormous 3-foot-diameter columns were two of the attractions of the loft space.

OPPOSITE: The designer built in a birch seating area in the corner of her dining room/library. A birch grid overhead effectively lowers the ceiling without blocking it.

PAGE 128: In the corner of her living room, Montgomery enclosed a space for her library and dining room.

PAGE 129: Montgomery resides in a building constructed in 1917 for the Ben Hur Coffee & Spice Company, located in the center of the Arts District.

COZY KITCHEN

To give her kitchen a more homey feeling, Montgomery "lowered" the room's 14-foot ceiling by way of visual tricks. She began by painting out the former industrial kitchen's exposed sprinkler system, fan vents, and plumbing, all of which she found unattractive. A coat of flat, dark, chocolate brown paint made them appear to recede. She then clad the kitchen walls in 8-foot-tall birch plywood sheets to establish a lower eye level. A 3-foot-wide slip-slot grid (echoing the one she used in the sitting area outside the kitchen) wraps the L-shape space. This dropped, partially open ceiling creates an illusion of the more traditional home-space ceiling height she desired. Both 6-inch square Mexican floor tiles and the ceiling grid are set at 30-degree angles to add more visual interest. She displays art and flowers in a wall niche illuminated with a recessed light.

ABOVE: Montgomery gutted former tenant Big Bang Café's kitchen and added new tile floors, birch cabinets, and a niche in the wall to hold flowers.

OPPOSITE: Craftsman Gustav Stickley chairs and table from Montgomery's former Spanish home are located in front of large windows that wrap the building. A built-in bookcase wall she added to the room serves as her library.

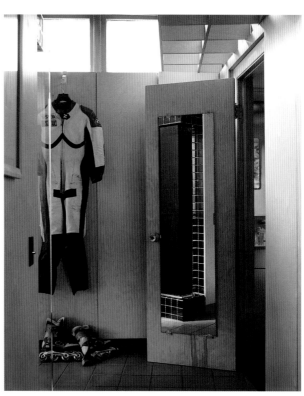

ABOVE: Montgomery sleeps behind 200-pound steel vault doors. (The locks have been dismantled so she can't accidentally lock herself in.) In order for her to sleep safely in the 10-by-20-foot room, it was necessary to drill a hole through the wall to bring in air and electricity.

ABOVE, RIGHT: Montgomery warmed up her vault bedroom with grass-cloth wallpaper and wall-to-wall carpet.

RIGHT: Adjacent to the kitchen, Montgomery added a bathroom, shower, utility room, and closets. Montgomery's motorcycle race suit hangs above her roller blades.

OPPOSITE: Montgomery's oak-trimmed entry was one of the features that sold her on the loft.

Home Brewery

KELLY REEMTSEN & DICK KOOPMANS

Painter Kelly Reemtsen and independent records design liaison Dick Koopmans live in a five-story concrete building overlooking Lincoln Heights that for a quarter century was home to the Pabst Brewing Company. Transformed into artists' lofts in the early 1980s, the premises still speak of their brewery past; a black stenciled designation on the bedroom door proclaims it to be "Fermenter/Storage Cellar J-11." At parties, Reemtsen and Koopmans serve Pabst Blue Ribbon beer in the can, which Reemtsen fittingly calls "our local home brew."

Other traces of the east L.A. brew plant remain: Gouged ceiling joists mark the spot where large steel vats once were attached. The scored, concrete floor has a definite slant. Reemtsen recalls setting a bowling ball on the floor and having it roll all the way to the kitchen where a floor drain used to be. The drain still is visible in the living-quarters half of the loft, which is divided evenly into two 1,500-square-foot spaces. The other half is Reemtsen's art studio.

The living space is mostly open: a reconfigured kitchen along the back wall; a dining room and den/library in the middle (where built-in shelves hold their 3,000-plus CD collection and books); and a curtain-enclosed guest bedroom and living room near the large front window. A former tenant—an architect—enclosed the bedroom next to the kitchen with a corrugated plastic, pyramid-shaped roof. Otherwise, says Reemtsen, the whole place would be open.

Adding ultraviolet shades to the 15-by-15-foot windows in each of the spaces was the first order of business when the couple moved in five years ago. (The windows had been installed after the initial building renovation, which breached the walls to remove the large brewing vats.) Although early morning light is good for painting, Reemtsen says, in summer it's 90 degrees by 9 a.m.

Reemtsen equipped her studio with a large printer, a pair of easels, and several large tables—all on wheels, so she can move things around depending on what she's working on. A grouping of Eames chairs from a Kaiser hospital waiting room face the window and overlook a large billboard which, Koopmans says, usually displays a beer ad.

One challenge for the young couple was simply furnishing the loft's yawning space. "We had a dining table but no chairs, a mattress, and a '50s bar when we moved in," Reemtsen recalls.

Now the loft is filled with their colorful midcentury furniture and fashion collections, also the subjects of Reemtsen's still-life paintings: Eero Saarinen pedestal chairs, Rudi Gernreich cocktail dresses, Capobianco platforms, vintage handbags. "I wear the dresses and shoes, carry the purses, and sit in the chairs. Then I paint them for posterity. Living here is a real art-in-life experience," Reemtsen says. "And having our own vintage home brew does have a certain cachet."

ABOVE: The painted concrete floor and ceiling beams still bear marks where vats once sat. "The floor has a definite slant to it for drainage," Koopmans says. "If we put a chair with casters by the window it will slide down toward the kitchen. You can still see the drain in the floor."

OPPOSITE, TOP: Against a weathered wall, Reemtsen placed a pair of colorful vintage dresses and a still-life painting of her kitchen's Eero Saarinen pedestal chairs.

OPPOSITE, BOTTOM: The couple reconfigured the kitchen cabinets along the back wall of the living-quarters side of the loft.

PAGE 136: A midcentury hutch full of Russell Wright dishware stands in front of the couple's enclosed bedroom, which is topped with a corrugated-plastic pyramid ceiling.

PAGE 137: A bridge links two concrete buildings at the Brewery, which was once home to the Pabst Brewing Company.

ABOVE: A long corridor marks the entrance to Reemsten's art studio.

RIGHT: Charles Eames chairs, which the couple purchased at the Santa Monica Antique Market, face a view of Lincoln Heights and a rooftop billboard that frequently advertises Corona beer.

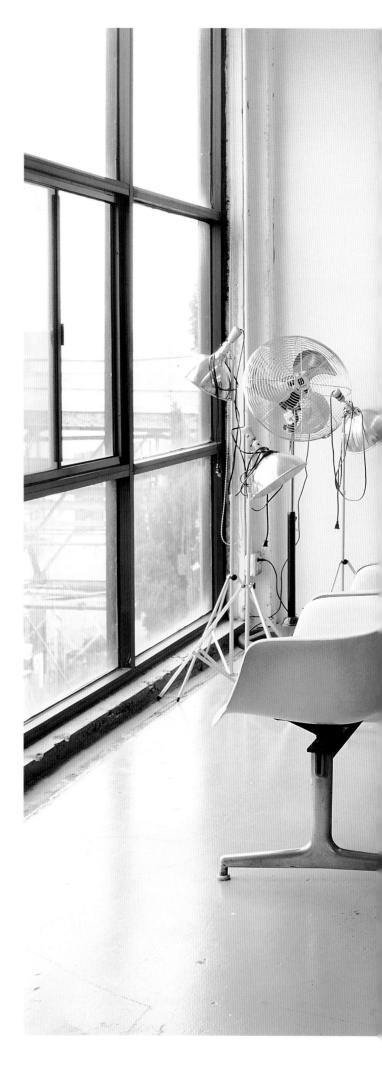

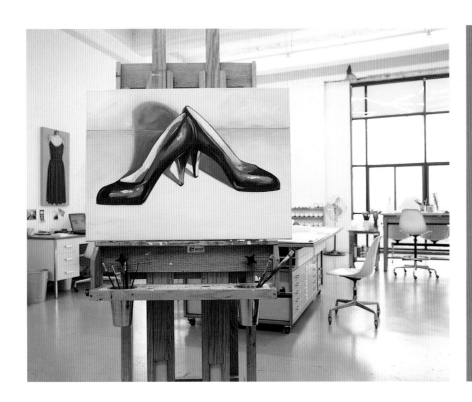

ON THE SHELF

Reemtsen needed bookshelves to hold her extensive vintage catalog and monograph collections and racks for more than 3,000 CDs. She selected the 6-foot-wide return wall facing away from the floor-to-ceiling window, she says, because sunlight can ruin books, drying them and making them brittle. The 15-foot-high wall allowed for nine shelves. To accommodate varying sizes of art books and vinyl records, she spaced the shelves at heights of 12, 13, and 16 inches. She made the cases in four 2-shelf sections, attaching each to wall studs with wood strips on the back. Keeping the shelves mounted slightly away from the wall allowed electrical cords to run down the back. An adjacent wall accommodates three CD rack bays; these are secured to the concrete floor with industrial-strength epoxy. All the shelves are painted white to blend with the loft walls.

ABOVE, LEFT: An easel-on-wheels features a painting of vintage blue pumps that Reemtsen made for the Mandalay Bay hotel in Las Vegas. A small office area, sandwiched between two sliding doors connecting the studio with the living quarters, is located to the left. Reemtsen keeps all the tables on wheels for easy mobility.

RIGHT: A Charles Eames La Chaise stands in front of Reemtsen's towering built-in bookcase.

PREVIOUS SPREAD: An orange curtain in the living room partitions off a small guest bedroom/storage room and sometime office for Koopmans.

Industrial Zen

JOE STURGES

Until a front entrance was added to his upstairs loft four years ago, sculptor Joe Sturges could only get to it through an art gallery. The two-story blue-brick building, a half-century-old one-time furniture warehouse, is located at the edge of the Arts District on Alameda Street.

His neighbors include a cold-storage locker down the block and an onion-storage facility behind the building. "When it gets hot," Sturges says, "there's a strong smell of onions in the air."

An Art Center School of Design graduate, Sturges moved to the 3,200-square-foot loft in 1995 from a Craftsman home in Pasadena. "The loft offered me a creative environment with room for a workshop that I could afford," he explains. "A lot of art students finish school, move into a small one-bedroom apartment and don't make art anymore."

When he moved in, Sturges recalls, he camped out in his backpacking tent in the corner of the loft, the current site of his bedroom. There was a kitchen and an enclosed bedroom and bath, and a couple of wall partitions in the living room; otherwise, the space was open. Occasionally, inquisitive art patrons wandered in. Says Sturges: "I wanted to take the time to feel and perceive the space and how I wanted it to unfold."

He began by creating a master bedroom sanctuary, complete with a recessed-niche Buddha wall and a built-in platform bed. He installed a diagonal wall between two existing walls to separate the bedroom from his open-plan office/kitchen/living room space. Three shelves built into the wall hold objects that contain meaning for Sturges: an urn with his grandfather's ashes, books on mysticism and Zen masters, and objects from his travels to Thailand and Indonesia.

He took a sledgehammer to the 1980s-style industrial steel shower with a faux-marble finish exterior, replacing it with a serene indoor-outdoor shower of corrugated metal and glass, and then added a reed screen backdrop and a small Asian-inspired garden. "I wanted to create a symbolic space that related to the natural environment, even though I'm in the middle of downtown," he says.

Opposite the bath, Sturges built a large workshop to make sculptures and furnishings for his company, Temple Designs, which specializes in creating personalized spiritual environments. Initially, the upstairs space served as a painting studio for a roommate, but it now functions as a guest bedroom.

Sturges's ethereal wood sculptures are placed throughout the space, bathed in light by a row of east-facing factory windows and a west-side clerestory. The aged concrete floor acts as a perfect foil for the artist's thrift-shop furnishings, done up in an earth-tone palette of fabrics.

Occasionally, Sturges drops down to the gallery and selects a painting to hang. "I've had an Ed Moses and a John Baldessari; right now there's a paper collage by Charles Hill hanging over the sofa," he says. "Living in a loft above a gallery, and being friends with the owner, has some definite perks."

ABOVE: Sturges added a floor-to-ceiling panel to divide the living area from his office space. Windows pivot open, bringing in natural light and, on hot summer days, the smell of onions from an onion-storage facility behind the building.

OPPOSITE, TOP: The loft is upstairs from Cirrus, one of downtown L.A.'s early art galleries.

OPPOSITE, BOTTOM: A tall pine sculpture by Sturges stands atop the loft's concrete floor.

PAGE 146: A ladder leads to an upstairs guest bedroom; below is Sturges's working studio.

PAGE 147: Sturges's loft is located in a two-story blue-brick building at the edge of the Arts District.

ABOVE: Sturges added a wall with a niche for a Buddha statue and a built-in platform bed to create his master bedroom sanctuary.

OPPOSITE: The kitchen sports a back wall of industrial terra-cotta brick painted black; overhead, another Sturges sculpture keeps company with his pots and pans.

PREVIOUS SPREAD: Sturges blended thrift-store furnishings with his own wood sculptures in the living area, which features a bank of industrial steel-frame windows and a weeping mortar wall.

INTERIOR GARDEN

Sturges created a sanctuary by building a small Asian-inspired garden next to his new corrugated metal-and-glass bathroom. Bamboo reed fencing material screwed into a frame forms the 6-and-a-half-foot-high backdrop. Atop the concrete floor he built a wooden casing lined with black plastic to contain black Mexican river stones. Towering bamboo stalks are mounted to plywood blocks and held in place by the weight of the stones. Nearby, a braided money tree (*Pachira aquatica*) grows in a terra-cotta pot. He cast two concrete stepping-stones for each corner of the space, one cut into the clear redwood floor. "They allude to a larger garden," he says, "like steps in a path." A redwood bench across from the 5-by-7-foot mini-garden offers a quiet space to relax and contemplate the symbolic landscape.

ABOVE: A large window from a salvage yard forms the partition between the shower and an Asian-inspired indoor garden.

OPPOSITE: Sturges added a corrugated metal shower and walls with a slate floor. The artist fabricated the storage cabinets around the stainless-steel sink, which he purchased from a local salvage yard.

Art-Park Atelier

DR. AVO TAVITIAN

A vast garage, really a 3,000-square-foot indoor parking lot, gives Dr. Avo Tavitian's loft in Atwater Village a special cachet. But what really sets the garage apart is that the owner, a gastroenterologist whose avocation is photography, uses it as an airy exhibition space. Tavitian converted the upstairs, once occupied by an alarm and security company, into a living space.

"I always wanted to live in an open, uninterrupted space," Tavitian says. "A loft is such a completely functional space. In many homes you never use the living room. Here, you use every inch." He began by removing the walls of four offices along the east-facing wall to create one spacious expanse, then painted and polished the sea-of-concrete floor a latte-hued beige. Horizontal bands of windows on the east and west sides of the room flood the interior with light; Tavitian also added eight rows of adjustable track lights to a ceiling already crowded with trusses and air-conditioning ducts. Islands of furniture define the living, dining, and sleeping zones. He employed a neutral palette of cream with bark and black accents.

Taking advantage of the existing plumbing, Tavitian installed a Poliform kitchen in the same location as the security company's former kitchenette near the top of the front entry stairs. He opted to keep the original office bathrooms adjacent to the kitchen "as a souvenir of their past life," he explains, adding, "The doors still have signs: Mens and Ladies."

On the opposite side of the loft, he added a semi-enclosed master bathroom with a large tub and glass-enclosed steam room and shower. Outside the bathroom, clothes hang casually from rows of metal apparel racks near the bed. Windows are covered in inexpensive paper shades. "The whole idea of a place like this," he says, "is to spend as little money as possible."

A quaint, tree-lined neighborhood of bungalows from the '20s, '30s, and '40s, Atwater Village is a small community situated next to Los Feliz on the edge of Griffith Park. The doctor, who grew up in a small Armenian neighborhood in east Lebanon, liked the idea of "a neighborhood in transition where I could set down roots and get to know everyone." When a contractor told him about an available building in 2002, Tavitian looked at the property and made an offer the same day.

In 2003, Tavitian opened Enisen, a gallery to showcase the work of young artists, in a one-story brick structure off a small courtyard behind the parking garage. Art openings at Enisen can attract over 200 guests; inevitably, the party continues upstairs in Tavitian's sleek, minimalist loft furnished in Italian modern.

ABOVE: Tavitian removed the walls of four offices along the east-facing window wall to create one spacious expanse.

OPPOSITE: An upholstered beige Minotti bed stands against a textured cinder-block wall. From the open bedroom, Tavitian can observe the entire loft. "When I slept here the first time, the sheer volume of the space made me feel exposed," he says. "Now, I don't think I can go back to an enclosed area. Psychologically, my creative side is inspired by the openness."

PAGE 156: Italian modern sofas face west, overlooking the back courtyard and gallery. Friends often watch films on a screen mounted in the ceiling or play the piano while Tavitian cooks nearby.

PAGE 157: Tavitian painted the two-story cinder-block building a dark marine blue; a rusty Cor-Ten steel panel below marks the entrance to the garage.

ABOVE: A Minotti dining table and chairs are stationed on a dark brown Pony rug; above hangs a chandelier inherited from the former tenants.

LEFT: Tavitian installed a modern Poliform kitchen in the same location as the former-tenant security company's kitchenette to take advantage of the existing plumbing.

SPA TREATMENT

Originally the upstairs loft had two bathrooms—basic basin-and-loo office facilities—that didn't satisfy Tavitian. What he wanted was a luxurious private bathroom just off his bedroom. To avoid opening up the floor, he ran plumbing along the garage ceiling from the bathrooms next to the kitchen to the bedroom side of the loft. He installed a 6-foot-long tub with a custom concrete surround and a 10-foot-long concrete-enclosed steam shower. The shower, with concrete seats and wall niches for toiletries on each side, allows two people to shower at the same time. Six knobs in the middle control handheld European-style showerheads in the ceiling and side walls. Another control turns the room into a wet sauna. "If I want to, I can take a cold shower and a hot sauna at the same time," Tavitian says. "It's like being in my own spa."

ABOVE: Tavitian's clothes hang casually from metal apparel racks in the bedroom.

RIGHT: Tavitian's bathroom features a 10-foot-long glass-enclosed steam shower.

Ad Hoc Gallery

JOE TERRELL

Environmental designer, curator, and art consultant Joe Terrell lived in a downtown L.A. loft in the mid-1990s and was hooked by the experience. "There's no yard to mow, no maintenance," Terrell says. "It's a freer way of living." When he moved back to Los Angeles after a sojourn in Arizona, he started loft hunting.

This time, in contrast to his former L.A. home in an old produce warehouse on the mean streets of downtown, Terrell opted for a newly constructed loft four blocks from Paramount Studios, in a neighborhood of prop houses and post-production studios. Perched on the Hancock Park/Hollywood border, his new home is less than a mile from Larchmont Village. "I grew up in this neighborhood," he says. "It feels familiar and safe."

Still, the loft building he'd taken for his new home was a far cry from the 1925 Tudor-style house in which he grew up. The two-unit, cinder-block complex, set behind an industrial mesh-metal gate, houses 10 lofts and has a common access drive. The two-story lofts sit atop spacious 1,000-square-foot garages that some tenants have turned into art studios.

The door to one of these garages leads to a diamond-plated steel stairway along a cinder-block wall to Terrell's living quarters. Set under an 18-foot-tall ceiling, his kitchen, living room, bathroom, and office are flooded with light from the large, south-facing window. Upstairs, a mezzanine bedroom sits under exposed ceiling joists. A small deck off the bedroom overlooks the interior parking court. Terrell planted the deck with morning glories and a bed of dichondra to add a bit of green to the hard-edged industrial space.

The designer, the first tenant to occupy the loft and an acknowledged perfectionist, felt compelled to enhance the pristine space. The existing white walls had too much yellow, he thought, so he repainted them with three coats of architectural white. This created a gallerylike venue for his large personal art collection and classic modern furnishings.

Unhappy with the lighting, Terrell added $3,000 worth (his wholesale cost) of additional track lighting, outfitted with adjustable lamps, to highlight the art. The original reflector lamps cast amber-colored shadows, he says, and there weren't enough lamps to illuminate each piece of art; the developers had put in just enough to pass code and no more.

The loft's natural light from the floor-to-ceiling window and cinder-block walls posed other challenges. For privacy and to cut light in the bedroom, Terrell removed the Plexiglas rail behind the bed. Taking its place, a cherrywood panel now serves as headboard and rail.

Mesh-fabric roller shades installed over the window cut 80 percent of harmful ultraviolet rays and protect valuable artwork. To hang art on difficult cinder-block walls, rubber anchors with large bolts go directly into the grout. Photographs and works on paper are hung away from direct light.

Still more art hangs in the garage, Terrell's ad hoc gallery. Photographs of Native Americans by Ed Curtis and oil paintings by Christopher Cox hang alongside mountain and racing bikes. Roll-up industrial doors at both ends of the garage flood the space with natural light when open.

Does a car belong next to valuable artworks? Terrell keeps the garage floor squeaky clean and is comfortable with the arrangement. "I needed the space," he says. "Besides, it's nice to drive in, park my car, and be surrounded by art."

ABOVE: A Charles Eames surfboard coffee table does double duty as a dining table when Terrell has guests.

OPPOSITE: A small aluminum table with a pair of stools serves as Terrell's "cappuccino corner."

PAGE 164: Terrell filled his loft with his own modern furnishings and classic twentieth-century pieces. The perforated burgundy-hued leather sofa and cube ottomans were designed by Terrell. The 16-foot-high-by-12-foot-wide south-facing window is outfitted with scrim shades that cut 80 percent of harmful ultraviolet rays. The shades allow those inside to see outside without being distinctly seen themselves. Photographs and drawings are all framed with protective ultraviolet Plexiglas frames and hung out of direct sunlight.

PAGE 165: The pair of cinder-block buildings is located in a post-production district a few blocks from Paramount Studios. New two-story lofts sit atop spacious garages that some tenants use for personal art studios and offices.

BRING TO LIGHT

Joe Terrell begins every design installation by lighting the artwork. His extensive collection was displayed to greater advantage, he says, when he removed 18 of the R lamps set within the H7 reflectors the developers had installed in the dropped, dry-wall ceiling of his loft. He retrofitted the reflectors with 1410W integrated transformers, which take versatile M-16 focal lamps. "These capsule lights with halogen filaments give a pure honest light—as opposed to the amber light given off by R lamps," he says. "They don't mess with the art or your face. It's as true to natural sunlight as possible." He also added two 4-foot tracks in the sidewall soffits running the length of the condo to highlight artwork on the cinder-block walls. In some instances, multiple lights shine on a single piece of art. Two MR-16 spots and an MR-16 flood lamp illuminate a painting in the bedroom by Marc Katano. "One lamp floods it with light, two others accent different areas, adding a three-dimensional quality," Terrell explains. "Lighting art is about enhancing a piece to its best potential."

ABOVE: Terrell installed a home office at the rear of the loft, behind the living room, and appointed it with his custom laminate desks and shelving. Reference books in narrow bookcase units are suspended on cinder-block walls.

OPPOSITE: Terrell fashioned a cherrywood headboard that also serves as a railing. Bamboo floors below and pressed particle-board ceiling joists above add texture.

PREVIOUS SPREAD: The small galley kitchen features new appliances, gunmetal gray–painted MDF cabinets, and a granite countertop. An array of wooden vessels tops a file cabinet in the designer's office.

LEFT: Photographs by Ed Curtis and oil paintings by Christopher Cox hang alongside Terrell's mountain and road bikes.

OPPOSITE: Roll-up industrial doors at both ends bring in natural light to the 1,000-square-foot garage Terrell uses as an ad hoc gallery and bicycle storage area. A low partition of opaque acrylic and two-by-fours hides storage at the rear of the space. When the south-gate is up, Terrell sees the back of the Brothers Collateral Loans, Pawnbrokers to the Stars.

Demi-Loft

DANNY VALENZUELA & MATT HUTCHISON

It all started with Maxx, an eight-year-old, 15-inch-high beagle. Maxx's owners, Danny Valenzuela, a furniture sales representative and interior designer, and Matt Hutchison, a financial consultant, wanted to move from their 1927 cottage in Los Angeles' Mid-Wilshire District, but most of the places they looked at didn't accept pets. They were having breakfast downtown one Sunday when they read about a new loft development nearby in the Old Bank District at Fourth and Main Street and decided to take a look.

They were impressed with the 1907 San Fernando Building. The newly painted building—an ivory field with rows of windows and cartouches highlighted in terra-cotta—with a dramatic marble staircase in the lobby appeared crisp and inviting. The financial-offices-turned-apartment-lofts featured brand-new, slate-clad bathrooms and galley kitchens. The units also had typical loft elements Valenzuela and Hutchison admired: concrete floors, tall ceilings, and a long row of windows. The unobstructed top-floor view of city hall and the snowcapped San Gabriel Mountains, and the fact the owners accepted pets, says Valenzuela, clinched the deal.

They rented a one-bedroom apartment on the eighth floor. But downsizing their living space from a three-bedroom, two-bath, 1,600-square-foot home to a space half the size proved challenging. They added a large, freestanding closet in the small bedroom for some additional storage, but mostly, Valenzuela says, "if we hadn't used it or touched it for over a year, we got rid of it. We did a major housecleaning."

The main room reflects Danny and Matt's pared-down approach to living. They designated the space opposite the kitchen as a living room, but what they really needed was a larger dining area for their frequent dinner parties. So when a 200-square-foot reception area across the hall became available, they leased that too, and turned it into a comfortable lounge. Their former living room is now a dramatic dining area.

Philippe Starck's snow-white slipcovered Lord Yo chairs surround Valenzuela's 7-foot-long white lacquered dining table. A twin mattress banquette with over-stuffed cushions along the wall serves as comfortable dinner seating and doubles as a daybed. Above, inexpensive flea-market picture frames are filled with sheets of chartreuse-colored Plexiglas to match the kitchen wall's Anjou pear hue.

Except for a blue accent wall in the bedroom, Valenzuela kept the rest of the space plain vanilla. "The loft is really a blank canvas for us," he says. "I can alter the mood just by changing accessories." When they host an Asian evening, he substitutes red Plexiglas in the frames, places shrimp ginger in vases, and sets the table with red napkins and wine glasses on bamboo placemats. "It gives the room a whole new personality."

The urban lifestyle agrees with the couple, although Hutchison says the lack of green space is sometimes vexing. "On the other hand," he points out, "there's no yard to take care of." And Maxx? "He's a completely urban pooch now. He loves the streets of L.A."

ABOVE: The demi-loft features a built-in galley kitchen with a pear green accent wall. A two-tiered restaurant console serves as a bar and casual eating area perfect for coffee in the morning.

OPPOSITE: The building features a dramatic white marble staircase entry with a graphic black-and-white ceramic tile floor.

PAGE 174: Valenzuela and Hutchison's 200-square-foot space across the hall has become their living room and cocktail lounge.

PAGE 175: The San Fernando Building, located in the heart of the Old Bank District on South Main Street, was one of the tallest buildings in Los Angeles when it was built in 1907.

FRAMES UP

Valenzuela added texture and enlarged his small space by hanging a dozen vintage picture frames holding colored Plexiglas and mirrors. The frames, purchased at garage sales and flea markets, range in size from 5 by 7 inches to 36 by 38 inches. He repaired any cracks with wood putty, then scrubbed the frames with a wire brush, soap, and water to remove dirt. To ensure a smooth, consistent surface, he sealed the frames with paint sealer before spraying them white. Clear yellow Plexiglas sheets the size of the interior frames are attached with a drop of hot glue in each corner (so they pop out easily when he changes color). He hung the frames gallery style, arranging them first on the floor in front of the wall in the desired composition. He began by hanging the largest, a mirror, in the lower right-hand corner, then continued from right to left, keeping the top row at the same height to establish visual order.

ABOVE: Borek Šípek's Simon candelabra adorns Valenzuela's white laquered dining table.

OPPOSITE: A custom white-lacquer dining room table designed by Valenzuela is surrounded by Philippe Starck Lord Yo chairs and a banquette for commodious dining. Inexpensive vintage frames add texture and color to the room.

The bedroom is just big enough for the couple's California king-size bed—but not a lot more. The wall space above the built-in closet is a display area for their collection of rosaries and lightweight foam busts.

Mini Hearst Castle

MAGNUS WALKER & KAREN CAID

In a word, British-born fashion designer Magnus Walker's warehouse loft is surreal. He calls it his "mini Hearst Castle." Indeed, you might think you have stumbled into a mothballed set for *Citizen Kane*; gargoyles are juxtaposed with stained-glass church windows and faux medieval sconces hang by Gothic doors. "My mum used to haul us kids around to see the grand English estates and castles," he says. "I guess it inspired me."

Walker and his wife, Karen Caid, weren't looking to live downtown. But in 2001, when they relocated their novelty clothing company to a two-story brick warehouse on the edge of the Arts District, they had more than enough space to make it their home as well—26,000 square feet, to be exact. The only drawback was that the 1906 building, just a few blocks west of the Los Angeles River, was in a gritty, asphalt jungle.

Whatever reservations the couple might have had were dispelled after they saw the 12-foot-high ceilings, hardwood floors, and skylights—not to mention the 1950s warehouse addition that was perfect for storing their collection of muscle cars. So, despite windows draped with garbage bags and skylights caked with tar, Walker and Caid set out to remake the loft above their first-floor office and production facility. They cleaned the skylights and added even more windows along the east and west walls to flood the interior with natural light.

To remove almost a century of grime, they stripped the floors and sandblasted the masonry and open-truss ceiling. Then they carved the cavernous space into intimate living quarters. They divided the loft with a brick wall into nearly mirror-image spaces; on one side, they added an enclosed kitchen, a dining room, a library, and a regal-sized master bedroom suite in railroad apartment fashion—the latter hidden behind a door worthy of a castle. On the other side, they put an enclosed guest bedroom and bath in the middle of the living room, because, Walker says, "we wanted guests to be at the center of everything."

The couple delights in spending time in their alley garden where sweet-scented jasmine and gardenias have replaced the graffiti. The green lawn and a gurgling fountain create a serene cloister—often rented by location scouts for movies and music videos. Says Caid, "You would never imagine from the front of the building that all this was here."

ABOVE: At the far end of the loft, a bank of windows and comfortable chairs create a cozy place to read.

OPPOSITE, NEAR LEFT: A large gargoyle, one of many scattered throughout the loft, adds to the Gothic castle ambience.

OPPOSITE, FAR LEFT: A modified Gothic-arch door worthy of a castle marks the entry to the guest bedroom, which the couple located off the living room.

PAGE 182: A stained-glass window from a church in Harlem acts as a colorful focal point in the couple's spacious master bedroom suite.

PAGE 183: The plain facade of the two-story brick building makes a good camouflage for the "mini Hearst Castle" inside.

ABOVE: Although they love their Gothic decor, the couple wanted a modern kitchen. An overhead skylight lights the enclosed space; blue fluorescents in clerestory-like windows add to the mood. Round wall niches echo the Op Art mirror and display Walker's guitar collection.

LEFT: The original slender white supports are now clad as substantial wood columns to further the castle theme.

OPPOSITE: A large, Gothic-style door marks the dramatic entry to the master bedroom suite. The walls wear a faux-finished, Old World patina.

PREVIOUS SPREAD: A new private entrance (far left) from the couple's enclosed garage into the living room allows them to bypass their workroom.

OLD WORLD GOTHIC

The couple wanted an Old World entrance to their master bedroom, so they had their French architect design a dramatic Gothic arch with a massive, red-stained glass door. The suite's walls were given an ocher hue reminiscent of an old abbey by being brushed with a flat, oil-based paint followed by a sponged glaze to create a mottled, antique effect. A pair of quatrefoils was cut out of the wall on either side of the door and a wood wainscot added below to enhance the effect. Fiberglass Gothic-style windows from the Rose Bowl flea market, medieval-looking metal sconces from Liz's Antique Hardware, and a stone gargoyle beside the door complete the look. The original spindly white posts throughout the loft have been transformed into hefty octagonal wood columns befitting a castle.

ABOVE AND OPPOSITE: The couple reclaimed a former graffiti-covered and rat-invested alley behind their loft and turned it into a green oasis.

BARBARA THORNBURG is senior editor of Home Design for the *Los Angeles Times Sunday Magazine*, where she writes and produces articles on home design, architecture, gardens, and entertaining. Prior to her writing career, Barbara worked as an interior designer in New York City and Los Angeles. She has served as president of the Los Angeles Conservancy, an umbrella-organization for Los Angeles' preservation community, and she has been active in several architectural preservation projects. Her work as a writer, producer, and stylist has appeared in publications such as *Metropolitan Home*, *Cosmopolitan*, and *Family Circle*. She is also a regular guest on television shows such as *The Christopher Lowell Show* and HGTV's *Rooms for Improvement*.

MICHELLE OGUNDEHIN is editor of *ELLE Decoration*. A veteran of *Tate Art Magazine* and *Blueprint*, she also runs her own interior design and creative direction consultancy. As a tastemaker and authority on design, she has contributed to publications all over the world, including *I.D.* magazine, London's *Sunday Times,* and *Numéro*. A native of Britain, Michelle has lived in New York, Los Angeles, and London and now makes her home in Brighton, England.

DOMINIQUE VORILLON is a French-born photographer who grew up near the Loire Valley and now calls L.A.'s Silverlake neighborhood home. His images of interiors and architecture appear regularly in American and European magazines such as the *New York Times Magazine*, *Architectural Digest*, and *World of Interiors*.